The Mind at Work and Play

Sir Frederic Bartlett

Routledge
Taylor & Francis Group

First published in 1951
by George Allen & Unwin Ltd.

This edition first published in 2025 by Routledge
4 Park Square, Milton Park, Abingdon, Oxon, OX14 4RN

and by Routledge
605 Third Avenue, New York, NY 10158

Routledge is an imprint of the Taylor & Francis Group, an informa business

Publisher's Note
The publisher has gone to great lengths to ensure the quality of this reprint but points out that some imperfections in the original copies may be apparent.

Disclaimer
The publisher has made every effort to trace copyright holders and welcomes correspondence from those they have been unable to contact.

A Library of Congress record exists under LCCN: 51007428

ISBN: 978-1-041-07759-6 (hbk)
ISBN: 978-1-003-64208-4 (ebk)
ISBN: 978-1-041-07760-2 (pbk)

Book DOI 10.4324/9781003642084

FIG. 1

The Mind at Work and Play

SIR FREDERIC BARTLETT
C.B.E., M.A., F.R.S.
Professor of Experimental Psychology in the
University of Cambridge
and Fellow of St. John's College

LONDON
GEORGE ALLEN AND UNWIN LTD
RUSKIN HOUSE FORTY MUSEUM STREET

FIRST PUBLISHED IN 1951

PRINTED IN GREAT BRITAIN
in 12 point Bell type
BY UNWIN BROTHERS LTD
WOKING AND LONDON

TO HUGH AND DENIS

FOREWORD

This book contains the substance of lectures, "adapted to a juvenile auditory," delivered at The Royal Institution during the Christmas season of 1948. Very little has been added and very little omitted. The only considerable change is in the style of presentation, which of necessity is less conversational and informal in the book than it was in the lectures.

It will be clear that all I have attempted to do is to select a number of topics, concerned with mental behaviour, and to show how they can be studied in simple experiments which are within the reach of nearly everybody. Whoever pleases—and it is my hope that many will—can carry out these experiments, and others that their results will suggest. He will find it an exciting adventure, taking him into territory that is still wide open to the scientific explorer.

I am deeply indebted to a large number of people without whose help these lectures could never have been successfully organized. Practically the whole research and workshop staff of the Cambridge Psychological Laboratory devoted much time to helping to devise experiments, to inventing and constructing apparatus, and in many instances they personally assisted in the demonstrations.

Particularly I wish to thank Mr. Bridger and Mr. Green of the staff of the Royal Institution, for the courtesy, understanding, and energy with which they helped to prepare all the practical arrangements for the lectures.

To my friends Professor H. S. Langfeld of Princeton University and Professor E. G. Boring of Harvard University, joint editors with Professor H. P. Weld of *The Foundations of Experimental Psychology*, my grateful acknowledgments are due for permission to use material from that book and from *The American Journal of Psychology.*

Finally, but for encouragement from the two to whom I have inscribed this volume, it is exceedingly unlikely that the work involved in its preparation would ever have been undertaken.

ACKNOWLEDGMENTS

Fig 1. is reproduced from *The World of Wonder* (New Series), edited by Charles Ray, by kind permission of The Times Publishing Co.

Fig. 7 is adapted by permission from suggestions made by Dr. Clifford Morgan, Director of the Psychological Department, Johns Hopkins University, U.S.A., and a group of associated psychologists.

The dial faces in Fig. 8 are adapted from a report on dial reading by Miss M. D. Vernon, now lecturer in Psychology at the University of Reading.

For Fig. 9 I am indebted to Chapanis, A., Garner, W. R., and Morgan, C. T., *Applied Experimental Psychology* (New York: John Wiley and Sons, 1949).

The experiment pictured in Fig. 12 was suggested by Dr. Paul Fitts of Wright Field, Ohio, U.S.A., and I am indebted to him for permission to refer to it here.

The instruments shown in Fig 13 were designed and built by Mr. C. B. Gibbs of the Medical Research Council Unit in Applied Psychology, University of Cambridge.

Fig. 16 is reproduced from *The Picture Magazine*, Vol. II, July to December 1893, p. 323, by kind permission of Geo. Newnes and Co., Ltd.

Fig. 17 is reproduced by permission of the author and the British Psychological Society from an article by O. Zangwill, Reader in Psychology, University of Oxford (*British Journal of Psychology*, Vol. XXVIII, p. 15).

Fig. 18 is reproduced by permission of the Cambridge University Press from my book on *Remembering*, p. 269 (Cambridge, 1932).

Fig. 19 is reproduced by kind permission of Professor E. G. Boring from the *American Journal of Psychology*, 1930, Vol. XLII, p. 444.

In connection with Figs. 20–22, see also *The Foundations of Psychology*, edited by E. G. Boring, H. S. Langfeld, and H. P. Weld, pp. 227–8 (London: Chapman and Hall, 1948).

The circuit in Fig. 25 was designed by Mr. A. Welford, Lecturer in Psychology, University of Cambridge. The experiment is adapted from a series of brilliant investigations carried out by Professor A. Michotte of the University of Louvain and described in *La Perception de la Causalité* (Louvain, 1916).

For Figs. 28–30 I am indebted to Mr. W. Adiseshiah, of the Cambridge Psychological Laboratory, who designed the original experiments in which they were used.

Fig. 31 is reproduced by kind permission of Professor E. G. Boring from the *American Journal of Psychology*, 1941, Vol. LIV, p. 437.

ACKNOWLEDGMENTS

Fig. 32: the late Professor M. Wertheimer introduced this puzzle to a group of American psychologists and my attention was drawn to it by Professor E. G. Boring of Harvard University, who also pointed out its difference in principle from cases of the *Horse and Rider* type.

Fig. 33: for reminding me of this problem and for producing the designs I am much indebted to Mr. G. C. Grindley, Lecturer in Psychology, Cambridge University.

CONTENTS

CHAPTER ONE

The Mind as a Measuring Instrument

I. ABSOLUTE MEASUREMENT

1. MEASURING DISTANCE

Everybody must have discovered that there are many things that it is perfectly easy to do in one way, but far less easy to do well in a different way. Take judging distance, for example. All able bodied persons in the world do this many times a day, sufficiently well for all practical purposes. We do it repeatedly whenever we eat or drink, whenever we find our way along a crowded pavement without bumping into anybody, whenever we cross a street. Particularly we do it in all quick ball games. Then the eyes size up the distance; the brain flashes the message to the muscles; the arms, legs and body move and the ball speeds more or less near—if we are skilled, astonishingly near—to the spot required.

And yet, the moment we have to use the mind to find a number, in miles, or yards, or feet, or inches, or whatever unit we like to take, and to say what any particular distance is, we discover that it is nothing like as easy as it seems.

Take an object and get three or four people to stand in different positions a few yards away and estimate by eye the distance between it and them. Astonishingly few estimates will be correct, and the errors, sometimes of over-estimation, and sometimes of under-estimation will be much larger than most folks would expect.

Of course judging distances is in any case a complicated

business. For fairly near distances we have to have accurate control of the muscles that move the two eyes nearer together or farther apart, nearer for the nearer objects and farther apart for the more distant objects, up to about sixty feet. We must also bring into play the muscles which control the shape of the lens which everybody carries about with him in each eye, flattening it out when the distance is greater and bunching it up when the distance is less. And of course both sides of the brain are active all the time; and all these processes have got to fit into one another, each playing its part at precisely the right moment.

Talking of two eyes, there is an experiment which anybody can do very easily. Place a board flat on a table with its near edge projecting so that even a light touch will knock it over. Then take a coin—a penny will do—and balance it flat on the projecting part of the board so that the coin's near edge too has no support. Now let somebody stand a few feet from the table, facing the coin. He must cover one eye completely and then, with right or left arm and forefinger fully extended in front of him, walk rapidly up to the table and as soon as he thinks he is at the right distance, without hesitating and with a single downward flick of the arm, knock the penny from the board with the tip of his forefinger, touching only the projecting edge of the coin. Nobody will do it successfully, except by chance, unless he has had a lot of practice; but with both eyes open any person with normal vision will find the task extremely easy.

With great distances the nature of the task changes. Eye movements and the shape of the lens have now little to do. We have to depend largely upon what we have learned and can remember about the actual sizes of objects. The clearness or haziness of the atmosphere has a tremendous influence, and we can get a lot of useful information when the object whose distance we are trying to judge is partly obscured by other objects between it and us. If the object we are looking at is unfamiliar, and there is nothing partially to block our view of it, especially when the atmospheric conditions are out of the ordinary, the eyes and the mind can make very large errors indeed in their estimation of long distances. Look at the accompanying picture (Fig. 1, frontispiece). It is a photograph of a canal tunnel, and the small white circle in the distance is one end of the tunnel. Make a guess at the distance from the end at which the photograph was taken.[1]

Without a great amount of experience it is impossible to estimate far distances anywhere near accurately, especially in flat country, over the sea, against the sky, or when the weather is clear or hazy.

2. LENGTH AND HEIGHT

Suppose we take a very much simpler task, the estimation by eye of the length of a single horizontal line. Look at the instance on the following page (Fig. 2) and, without using any additional measuring aid, judge its length.[2] Or better still take a fairly large sheet of blank paper. Draw on it a single horizontal line, not exactly in the middle, and get a number of people to say how long it is. Different attempts will be found to vary much one from another and very few of them to be exact. Estimates made in the same way of the height of a vertical line will be found in general to vary even more.

3. POSITION

On the face of it, to identify a single position seems as if it should be an easier task still. To discover something definite about this take a blank sheet of paper quarto size.

[1] The correct answer is given on pages 34–5 and the results which were obtained when this picture was shown in the Christmas Lectures are summarized there.

[2] For information concerning this see page 36.

Fig. 2.

Put a small black dot on it, not exactly in the middle, or on the line of either of the diagonals. Let somebody have a single short glance at the sheet with its dot, for not more than a brief fraction of a second, Then, 15 seconds later, give him another blank sheet of paper, the same size as the first and ask him to put a dot on it in the identical position as nearly as he can estimate. Take his attempt and show it to a third person and in exactly the same way get another identification of this second position on a third sheet, allowing the same interval of 15 seconds between observation and assignment. Carry on the series, with a fresh person for each attempt, for as long as you like. Then, superimposing the second sheet on the original one, mark the position of the first assigned spot, with a pin, on the first sheet. Do the same for all successive estimates, and join the perforations on the original, with little arrow heads to mark their order. This will produce what we can call a Map of the Wandering Dot. Here are two actual maps obtained in this way (Fig. 3) and it will be seen, not only that the dot wanders, but that in these cases, with occasional small returns, the direction of its wandering remains constant. Very much still remains to be discovered about the wandering of dots or other small objects whose position has to be reported by observers when the original is seen for a short time only. In general, assigned positions seem to drop, or rise, towards the nearest boundary in the visual field. It would be particularly interesting to replace the dots by tiny arrow heads or by little lines thick at one end and thin at the other and to see whether the direction of their wandering can be controlled.

Next, try varying the interval between the observation and the attempted identification of position. It will be found that an increase of interval of, or above, half a minute, very greatly increases the wandering, and this is extremely interesting in view of some of the things that we shall learn later about remembering (see pages 96–7).

The estimation of positions of dots and other small objects has become of great importance in the world in which we live, for it has frequently to be attempted in

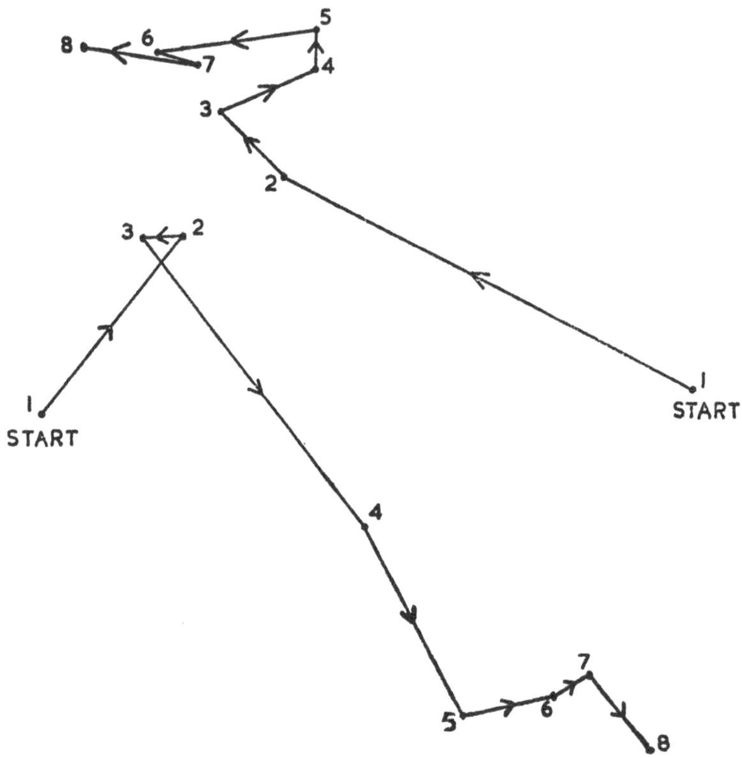

FIG. 3.

radar and other displays used for one purpose and another. If we carry out this simple-looking experiment systematically and fully, we can discover much that will not only be interesting about how the mind deals with positions in space, but also much that may be of practical value as well.

Science cannot be exact without accurate measurement, and the measurements that are needed must be available in some way that can be read off by an observer accurately and usually without any delay. The experiments that we have just carried out have shown us that the human senses and the human mind are not very good absolute measuring instruments in the case of distance, length, height, and position. If we had tried anything else that the senses can tell us about, the brightness of lights, the loudness of sounds, the weight of objects, the speed of movement, the smoothness or roughness of surfaces, or anything that is measurable in smell or taste, we should have discovered exactly the same state of affairs. Yet these are all things that people obviously can deal with, and are dealing with quickly and well, somewhere or other, every moment. So let us now do all our experiments over again, in a different way.

II. RELATIVE MEASUREMENT

1. POSITION

Take another sheet of blank paper, quarto size, and this time draw in a number of one-inch squares covering the whole area. Now put a dot in the same sort of position as before, carry out the experiments exactly as already described, and get a few more maps of the wandering dot. It will at once become evident that the errors are greatly reduced. Here, for example, is a map obtained from eight successive observers on a squared paper (Fig. 4). In this case the dot moves out of the original square, but by very little, and often it will wander even less. It is interesting to try different designs of grid background. For every shape or size of object whose position must be estimated there is some design of grid which gives the best results, but not much is known about this. And what about using a more and more finely meshed grid, more and more, and smaller and smaller, squares, for example? We shall find that after a certain point, the capacity of any single box, in a network of boxes, to control the wandering of the dot, is lost. Some of the reasons for this will become clear later

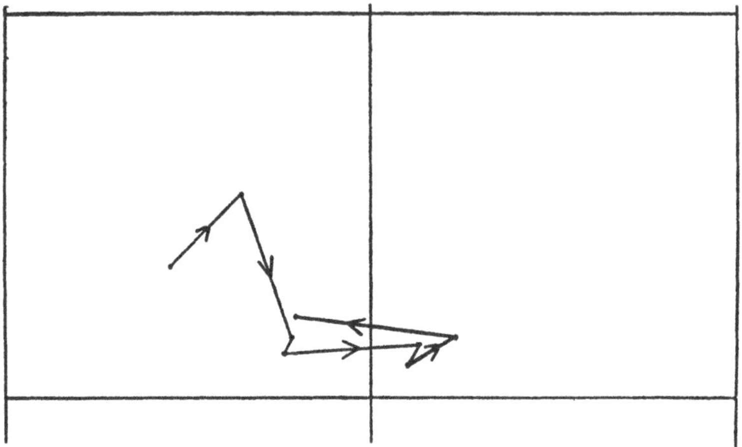

FIG. 4.

on (see p. 24). In general, however, we have now found that a given position can be much more accurately estimated if we can compare it with standard fixed positions.

2. LENGTH AND HEIGHT

Look at the lines on the opposite page (Fig. 5). They differ in length, but are in mixed order. Each line has a number. Starting with the longest line, write the numbers to correspond with decreasing lengths, from the longest to the shortest.[1] This is easy enough, and people agree with one another astonishingly well, although the differences between any two lines lie well within the variations between the largest and smallest estimates in the case of any single line of comparable length. Exactly the same is true of relative heights.

3. DISTANCE

With a little ingenuity and the help of a couple of toy

[1] See page 37 for the correct order.

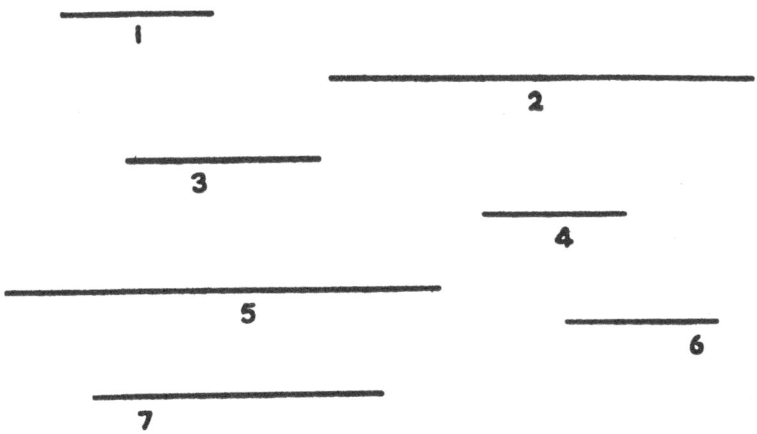

Fig. 5.

railway bogeys or trucks, and about eight or ten feet of toy railway line, anybody can easily construct a piece of apparatus which will show what must be done if near or moderate distances are to be judged exactly (see Fig. 6, opposite page). Erect on the trucks a wooden or metal rod about six inches high and tapering to a point at the top. At the far end of the railway line put a screen, painting it black or white so as to give the clearest and sharpest view possible of the top ends of the rods. At the near end of the line put up another screen with a horizontal slit at eye height so that an observer looking through the slit can see the tops of the rods but not the rest of the set-up between himself and the far screen. Now fasten to the rear of each truck a string which passes through a hole in the distant screen, and put a weight on the end of the string. Two other strings come from the front of each truck through a hole in the forward screen and out to the observer.

Set either truck in a fixed position and move the other nearer to or farther away from the observer, who will now let out or pull in the string until he judges that the two rod tips are exactly the same distance from him. Any observer with normal vision will be astonishingly exact. His accuracy will lessen somewhat as his distance from the rods increases, and of course with really great distances this experiment will not show the same result, for nothing but experience can improve accuracy very much in that case.

We have now reached the point at which we have found, by several experiments, that the senses and the mind can get along very well with measurement, if we provide some kind of fixed standard for comparison. Although this seems to be simple and obvious, it is still often forgotten by experimenters in scientific laboratories, and even more by "practical" people in everyday life. They very often believe that they can do a lot more than they

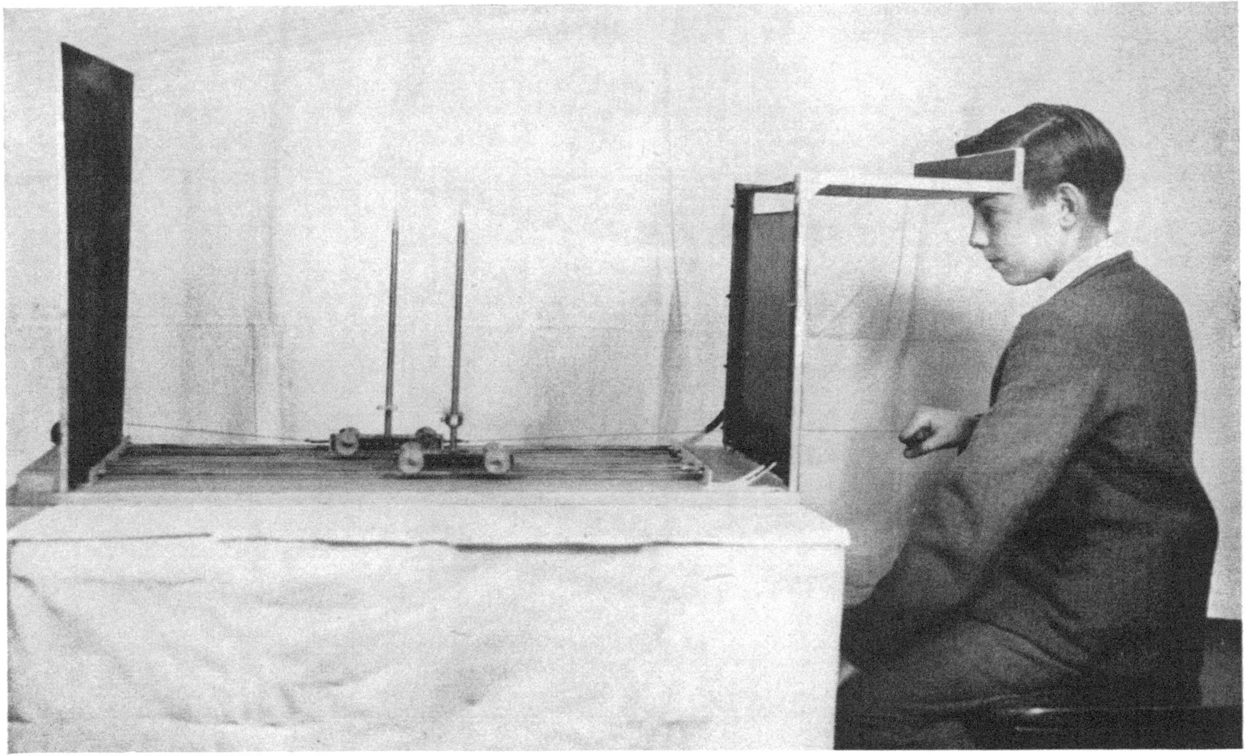

Fig. 6.

Fig. 10

really can in the way of direct and accurate estimates of sensory magnitudes, and they set their senses and minds jobs which these are very ill-designed to carry out.

All the common methods used for exact measurement involve the employment of variable magnitudes which can be related to standard positions or brightnesses or weights or whatever it is that is being considered. This is the natural outcome of the fact that absolute estimation of any kind of magnitude is apt to be unreliable. But merely realizing that is not enough to make accurate, and especially rapid, measurement possible. Standards and series of standards can be designed and represented in such a way that most observers will find it hard to deal with them. The same is true of whatever represents the variable; a moving pointer or spot of light, a varying size, colour, shape, direction or number. And the same is true of the relation between the varying value and the fixed standards. Unless all these are designed with a view to what the human senses and the mind can do naturally and well, merely to have instruments to help us to measure may produce more difficulties than it surmounts.

III. THE DESIGN OF MEASURING INSTRUMENTS

Obviously an extremely large number of questions arise when the design of measuring instruments is being considered. But if a few of the leading working principles of these are illustrated, anybody who sees their importance can easily work out for himself other things that ought to be safeguarded in any particular instance in which he is specially interested.

Because they are probably more widely used than any other type of instrument, we will take the cases of recording dials, and of vertical or horizontal scale columns, which can either be applied directly to objects, some character of which is to be measured, or which carry on themselves some recorder device.

It is often supposed that measures will be the more accurate the more fixed points for comparison are provided on a dial face or scale column. This is certainly untrue, especially if readings have to be taken quickly. Look at these two dial faces (Fig. 7) and try to read them at a glance. Everybody will at once agree that the easier one is not the one with the larger number of fixed positions of reference.

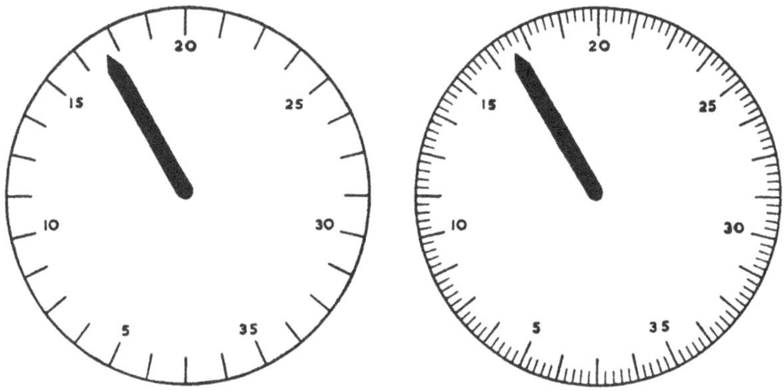

FIG. 7.

This is a particularly interesting instance, for it shows that the mind can be both quick and correct at filling up a gap. Filling a gap is, speaking generally, the most important thing that anybody does when he thinks, and this is, in fact, an elementary case of thinking which shows that the mind can do something in measurement, given a fair chance, more speedily and correctly when the eyes or other senses are relieved of a load of minute detail. (See also pp. 121–2.)

Look now at Fig. 8. The dial face at the top left corner contains the little-used feature of a gap between the maximum and zero readings, and can be compared with its fellow on the right. The value of a blank space of this kind depends on the fact that it is easier to notice a displacement of position than it is to notice the direction of the displacement. When a dial record must be read in a hurry it is not at all uncommon to find that a high value is mistaken for a low one or a low one for a high one unless some special device, like this gap, is used to draw attention to their difference.

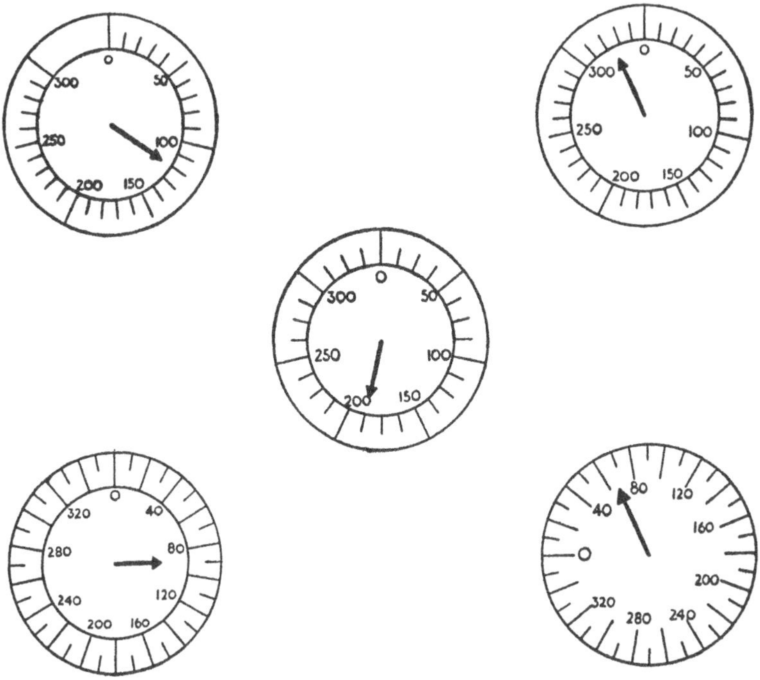

FIG. 8.

The remaining three dial faces all have one unsatisfactory feature in their design. In general, scales arranged in 4's and multiples of 4's lead to unnecessary errors. On the whole the best number interval is 1, 10, 100, and so on, with ten divisions between each pair of numbers. Scales of 0, 10, 20 and so on, with five divisions are also usually easy to read. The reasons why nearly everybody finds some number series, and some grouping of divisions between main numbers hard to deal with are not, as yet, well known. Experiments are not difficult to devise and carry out, and anybody with sufficient interest could find out many interesting facts about the type of scale design which best suits most readers, from the point of view of the main numbers and the arrangement of steps.

The bottom left dial face has one very bad feature. The pointer stops so far short of the scale numbers and divisions that exact estimation is extremely difficult. On the other hand, the bottom right design is bad because it has no internal circle and because the pointer is so long that it can actually obscure a number which it should directly indicate.

Now look at all five dials as a single set which may have to be dealt with altogether. This is a kind of thing that happens very often, as when a man is driving a car, piloting an aircraft, working in an engine room of a ship or a power house, or perhaps operating a switchboard; it is also necessary in many experimental situations in the laboratory. This particular set is a bad one, though it is nowhere near as bad as a great many that have to be used every day. It is bad because there is no constant principle of arrangement running through the whole set. Especially these dials vary both in their numbered steps and in the ways in which the spaces between the main points are divided. If scales must be varied it is better to keep the numerical system the same and to change only the number of steps within each main division. Worse still is the feature that one of the dial faces has been turned round so that, for example, similar pointer positions on the top and bottom right hand dials have entirely different values. The evidence is that fast reading of scales has little to do with intelligence, except when the dials are differently graduated, and then the more intelligent operators will be quicker and better. But there are plenty of other things which people who have to read dials and scales must do with their intelligence, and there is little sense in making operations hard just where they ought to be and can be easy.

There is a special case of the interpretation of banks of dials, or other scales, in which the important thing is not the precise reading on any one scale, but noticing at once whether any one or more of the pointers has moved beyond certain limits of safety. This is often the principal question for the air pilot, or the engine room operator, and it may be the case in numerous experiments. Look at Fig. 9A, and it is easy to see that when the mark which indicates safety limits (in this case a thick black line) occupies the same position on all the dials, it is very much simpler to see at a glance which pointers lie outside the safe area and call for correction. And when Fig. 9A is compared with Fig. 9B another thing is clear. For when horizontal scales—which in general are easier to read than circular ones, though for some reason or another they seem to be less popular—replace the dials and are ranged one under another, what is called "vernier acuity" (the visual perception of horizontal displacement) can come immediately into play. And so far as human eyes are concerned this is by far the most delicate and accurate of all ways of noticing small differences of position.

Enough has been said to show that while instruments are necessary if the human senses and mind are to get measurements accurate enough to be used for scientific purposes, those instruments must be designed with a constant regard for what most normal people can do well. This is a subject about which knowledge is still full of gaps, and any intelligent person can discover and demonstrate by experiment many new facts.

IV. SUCCESSIVE MEASUREMENTS

1. AFTER EFFECTS

Frequently measurements have to be made one after another. Sometimes the speed of successive measurements

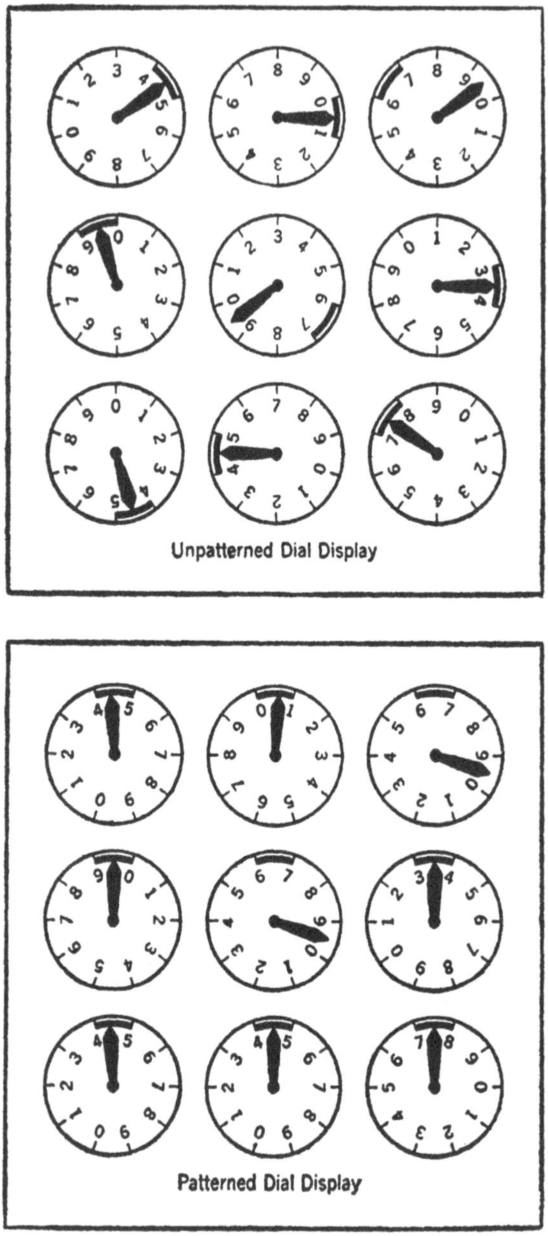

Fig. 9a.

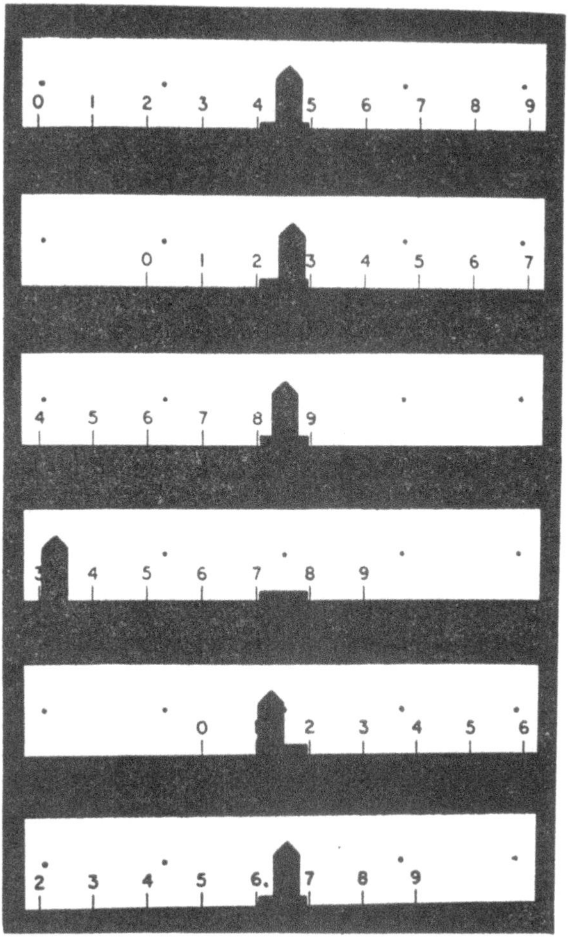

FIG. 9*b*.

depends upon the rate at which things happen in the outside world, and sometimes their speed can be directly controlled by the observer. In either case it is very important that we should know something about how, when the senses and the mind have done one job, they can be influenced by this, if they have to repeat the operation soon after, or do something else closely related to the first thing.

Take a stout piece of white cardboard about 24 inches by 20 inches. Paint a thick black vertical line exactly in the middle of the sheet and two other similar lines to right and left of the first, about 3 inches distant from it (Fig. 10, opposite page 23). Do the same with a second sheet. Now place the second sheet in a suitable framework so that it presents a flat vertical surface. Bend over the first sheet so that it is convex to an observer, and fix it to the same frame, with any arrangement, such as a hinge at the top, which makes it easy to remove the convex surface quickly, exposing the plane card behind it. Stand about 20 yards in front of this and look fixedly for 15 seconds at the middle of the middle black line of the convex surface. Then get somebody to remove the curved surface, exposing the flat vertical surface at the back. The plane surface will appear concave to observation, and will so stay for several seconds.[1]

Obviously if contours and surfaces have to be estimated in rapid succession one may distort another, and the same is true, within limits, of size, shape, weight, brightness and many other sensory magnitudes.

This happens to be a particularly interesting instance, about which much still remains to be discovered. If, for instance, the plane surface is left completely unmarked, when the convex one is removed the after-sensations of the three black lines will usually appear sharply defined upon the white background of the second card. In this case most observers report that the surface at the back appears either exactly vertical or only very slightly curved away from the observer. The after sensation is probably a retinal process, due principally if not entirely to some change going on in the eyes themselves whereas the apparent

[1] My attention was first called to this particular after effect by Professor W. Kohler, of Swarthmore University, U.S.A. I have chosen it as a leading illustration because very little is known about it, and it can be easily set up and tried by anybody.

curvature is a central interpretation due to something in the brain. Where the retinal effect is made obvious it seems to stop the central effect from being noticeable. But nobody knows why or how this is done, or whether it is a general principle or not. It does show, however, that there may be various ways in which after effects can be controlled in duration and amount, and it is important that these should be experimentally studied in many different instances.

Some after effects, particularly those concerned with colour, brightness and moving objects, are well known to everybody, but there are others, especially those which involve experiences of light pressure, of weight, and of bodily movement, which are far less known, but are important whenever measurements that rest partly upon them have to be obtained one after another. Anybody can think out for himself instances in which, for example, the width of objects must be judged by touch or light pressure when the actual widths dealt with vary from thin to thick; or when measurement depends on returning a limb to a given position after it has moved away from that position for a while; or when to get a required measure an amount of resistance has to be overcome and then the same process or a very similar one repeated. These are all things that happen in everyday life, and also, on occasions, in the laboratory. In all these and many other cases there are after effects whose duration and influence are usually little considered; and in fact so far not much is known about them though the necessary experiments would not be difficult to devise or to carry out.

2. ANTICIPATION

Every physical training instructor and every drill sergeant knows, or at least has plenty of chance to learn, the big part that anticipation may play, for good or bad, in the control of the direction of movements that have to be carried out in a series. Similarly when a number of measurements have to be made in succession, each one with its appropriate sensory signal, whenever he can do so a clever observer will nearly always try to anticipate.

It is not quite so easy to demonstrate anticipation in measurement, its uses and its limitations, as it is to demonstrate after effects. But with a little ingenuity anybody can arrange an experiment and find for himself what happens.

Suppose we have to estimate successive positions of a "hand" or pointer revolving on a circular disc. It is a simple matter to draw a series of displays of this kind with the pointers in the different required positions, and to expose the discs singly, with the help of a regularly revolving drum, or a film strip with a suitable projector, at appropriate speeds. A normal observer with a little practice will take about half a second, or a little more, to deal with each item. Now make a bank or cluster of such discs and expose them all at once. Before long the observer will be found to be working a little ahead of the dial with which he is actually dealing at the time. He has some impression of the position of a pointer before he reaches it, and when he does reach it he is, so to speak, "triggered" to go off extremely rapidly. He can therefore deal somewhat more quickly with items when he has a whole cluster of them before him, but nevertheless must take them in succession, than he can with the same items when each is given by itself.

Naturally the gain is most marked when the items have a regular serial order; when, for example, the pointer moves around the disc in a constant direction and by a succession of equal steps. It is particularly interesting to find out what happens if the order is broken at some point. Maybe the break will pass entirely unnoticed, or maybe a little before the unusual item is reached hesitation sets in, the whole process is slowed up, and a number of errors of estimation may occur.

Even if there is no regular order of change in the successive items forward reading still occurs, especially with the more practised observers. The distance ahead at which normal people can work under these conditions—the "range of anticipation" as it is called—has not yet been properly established, but probably it is rarely more than two or three items. Speaking generally, anticipation, working in this way, increases speed; whether it increases or lessens accuracy depends mainly on the type and arrangement of the material that is being dealt with, and especially on the way in which successive items are linked together.

V. CONCLUSIONS

We can now sum up the main points which our experiments have demonstrated.

1. We found that the human senses, as they are controlled and directed by the central nervous system and the mind, are not at all reliable if they are required to estimate or measure single magnitudes of any kind.

2. Nevertheless, if they are given fixed standards with which the magnitudes can be compared, they become accurate within small limits of error.

3. This is the fundamental reason why all exact scientific measurement has to use instruments of various kinds, the principle of which is that the variable magnitudes which have to be measured can be compared with fixed values marked on the instruments.

4. Then we discovered that it is not enough simply to have instruments which provide standards for comparison. Such instruments can be, and often are, designed in such a way that the senses and the mind are bound to find the comparisons that are demanded very difficult to make, and

then serious errors of measurement are bound to occur. Our special experiments were concerned with circular and other forms of scale, and we found that much depends on the number and arrangement of scale divisions; on the type and length of pointer, or other recorder device, that is used; and when banks or clusters of scales are used, on finding an arrangement which makes the comparison of one scale with another easy and correct. Similar problems arise whatever other special type of measuring instrument has to be employed, but once we grasp the principle that there are some kinds and arrangements of signals that the senses and the mind can interpret readily and correctly and other kinds of signals and arrangements which theoretically can be used for precisely the same purposes that are usually interpreted with difficulty and error, experiments to settle what design is the best one can be made.

5. Lastly, we considered the special but common case in which measurements have to be made in succession, and we discovered two important facts. When the human senses do anything they very often start up a train of after-effects which last for some time, and may, unless they are carefully controlled, or allowed for, interfere with what is done next. And further, when stimulus series are involved the human mind tends to run on ahead of the point with which it is specially dealing at any moment, and this anticipation may sometimes help and sometimes hinder exact measurement.

ESTIMATES OF ABSOLUTE LENGTH

1. The correct answer is that the photograph was taken from a distance of 7,040 yards (4 miles).

At the lecture 263 estimates were returned. These were distributed as indicated in the following histogram. It will be seen that estimates varied from 11 yards (the lowest) to 22,880 yards (the highest), and that the very large majority of them were under-estimations.

THE TUNNEL

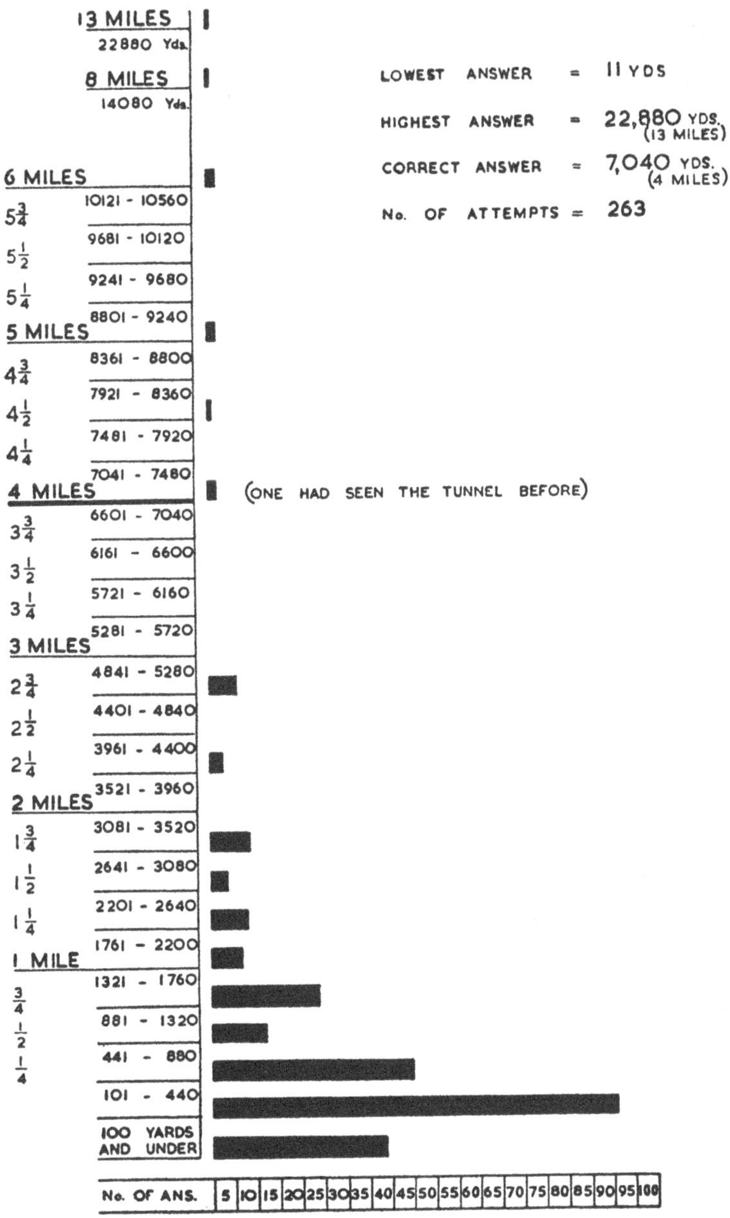
13 MILES
22880 Yds.
8 MILES
14080 Yds.
LOWEST ANSWER = 11 YDS
HIGHEST ANSWER = 22,880 YDS. (13 MILES)
CORRECT ANSWER = 7,040 YDS. (4 MILES)
No. OF ATTEMPTS = 263
6 MILES
$5\frac{3}{4}$
10121 - 10560
$5\frac{1}{2}$
9681 - 10120
$5\frac{1}{4}$
9241 - 9680
5 MILES
8801 - 9240
$4\frac{3}{4}$
8361 - 8800
$4\frac{1}{2}$
7921 - 8360
$4\frac{1}{4}$
7481 - 7920
4 MILES
7041 - 7480
(ONE HAD SEEN THE TUNNEL BEFORE)
$3\frac{3}{4}$
6601 - 7040
$3\frac{1}{2}$
6161 - 6600
$3\frac{1}{4}$
5721 - 6160
3 MILES
5281 - 5720
$2\frac{3}{4}$
4841 - 5280
$2\frac{1}{2}$
4401 - 4840
$2\frac{1}{4}$
3961 - 4400
2 MILES
3521 - 3960
$1\frac{3}{4}$
3081 - 3520
$1\frac{1}{2}$
2641 - 3080
$1\frac{1}{4}$
2201 - 2640
1 MILE
1761 - 2200
$\frac{3}{4}$
1321 - 1760
$\frac{1}{2}$
881 - 1320
$\frac{1}{4}$
441 - 880
101 - 440
100 YARDS AND UNDER
No. OF ANS.
5 10 15 20 25 30 35 40 45 50 55 60 65 70 75 80 85 90 95 100

2. The single horizontal line exposed for estimation at the lectures was 40 inches in length: 262 attempted estimates were returned, varying from $3\frac{1}{2}$ inches (lowest) to 108 inches (highest) and distributed as indicated in the following histogram. It will be seen that there are considerably more under- than over-estimations.

HOW LONG WAS THE LINE ?

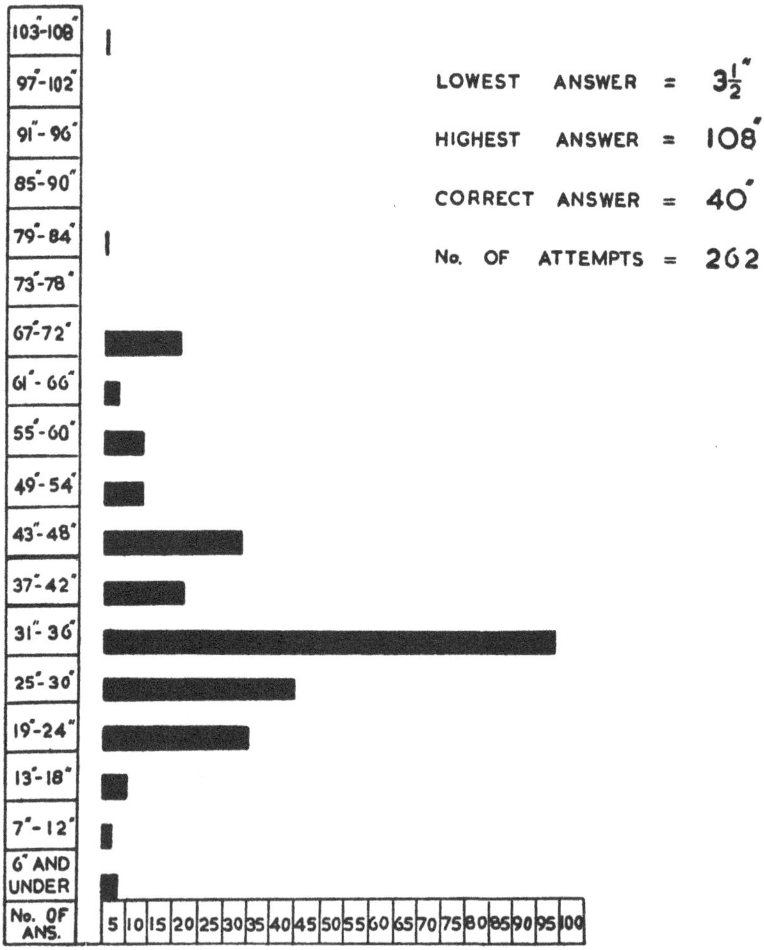

3. Lines of varying length.

Number of answers submitted . .	263		
Number of correct comparisons	114	43%	approximately.
Number with 1 error	88	33%	,,
Number with 2 errors . .	48	18%	,,
Number with 3 errors . .	10	4%	,,
Number with 4 errors . .	2	1%	,,
Number with 5 errors . .	1	1%	,,
	263	100%	

Correct order is: 5, 2, 7, 3, 1, 6, 4.

CHAPTER TWO

The Mind Controls Body Movements

Often in the laboratory, and almost always in everyday life, measurements have to be treated as signals for something else to happen. A pointer moves over a dial face; a spot or a line of light is seen in some special position on a cathode ray tube; a sound is heard to change in a particular manner; a wheel increases or slows down the speed of its movement. In each case the direction and extent of the change may have to be estimated, and then something must be done about it, a switch pressed or a brake applied, or another wheel rotated, or a lever pushed or pulled. To do these things bodily movements are needed, sometimes of one limb, but often requiring a combination of several parts of the body.

In these days machines have come to play a tremendous part in all scientific research and its applications. And it is particularly with machines that measurements lead on to movements. Since immense numbers of people spend the greater part of their waking lives designing, constructing, controlling and maintaining mechanical and electrical apparatus, it has become important to discover how these can best be done.

Every machine operator has to try to deal all the time with two great classes of problem. The machine gives him signals for action which he must notice and generally estimate or measure in some way. We have already considered how some of these signals should be designed. Together they form what is called the "display" of the machine, and we have seen that a satisfactory display must be designed with a view to what the senses and the mind can do well. In addition, the machine has its system of "controls" which bodily action is required to adjust. The controls also may be good or bad, and we can discover the differences between them only by experiments which will show us what sorts of movements can be made and combined by a normal person readily, accurately and with little strain or trouble.

Even if we consider the much freer situation in which most games are played the case is not radically different. The display now is the rapidly varying picture of the changing positions and relations of the players and of the materials of the game. The controls are the means which have to be used to manipulate the materials and much depends upon their being designed in such a way that the necessary manipulations can be produced rapidly, accurately and without a lot of unnecessary fuss.

We must, then, next look into the question of how controls can be so arranged as to fit in best with the kinds of bodily movements which the vast majority of ordinary people can learn to use without a lot of muddle. Of course this is a tremendously wide question, and all that can be done is to try to bring out a few principles and to illustrate them so that anybody who is interested can, if he wishes, find out more for himself. We shall be concerned almost entirely with machine-controlled movements because they are the simplest and easiest with which to illustrate the principles that need consideration.

1. THE POSITIONING OF CONTROLS

The first question that crops up is where we shall put our materials on a working bench, and what sort of a bench we shall use. Often this is decided for us because we have a limited amount of space, or have to use a particular sort of material. But there are many cases in which we have a fairly free choice, and then some principles are worth keeping in mind.

The problem of where to put material in, for example, an assembly operation is, in general, a fairly easy one, although in a large number of actual cases nobody ever thinks of it at all. Stand at normal working distance from the bench and, starting with the right hand near the left side of the body, describe an arc on the bench with the right arm fully extended but without changing the body position, or bending over in any way, moving the arm from left to right. Do the same with the left hand, starting from the right side of the body, and moving from right to left. The overlapping portion of the two arcs indicates working positions equally good for either hand. Outside the overlapping portion, the inner half of either arc is the best working area for the right or left hand alone. The outer halves of the areas are possible working positions for either hand alone, but are less good. The working materials can now be arranged with these guiding rules in mind, and positions outside of the areas will be used only when it is necessary in order to get over the even greater difficulties of inconvenient crowding.

What about the plane of the surface on which we dispose tools, or materials, or controls? Here again practical considerations of space or lighting may leave us no choice. But often enough to make it worth considering, a broad choice between a horizontal, or an inclined, or a vertical surface is possible. The best thing is to try an experiment. Prepare three working boards marked out with arcs as suggested, one to be used as a flat horizontal surface, like a table, another inclined to an angle of about 45 degrees, and the third as a vertical panel. Fix thirty to forty hooks in similar positions on each board all lying in the inner or outer halves of the arcs. Fix two wooden or metal studs to each board at the bottom, and in the middle of the overlapping arc areas, and slip as many rings as there are hooks over the studs, an equal number on each stud. (See Fig. 11, opposite page 48.)

Now take three people, preferably of about the same height, one to work on each surface. At a given signal each operator picks up *one* ring at a time and places it over any hook he likes, using the left hand for rings on the left stud and the right for those on the right stud. He has to go as fast as he can, and, when he has disposed of all the rings, to replace them one at a time finishing the task with everything as it was to begin with.

This is usually sufficient to demonstrate that the vertical panel is more difficult to deal with than either of the others. If the experiment is kept going for several complete trials without rest, and especially if the inclined plane is made adjustable, it can be shown that for most operators an inclined plane is the best, the flat surface next best, and the vertical arrangement the worst.

Here we have our first illustration of how movements which have to be made from the shoulder and involve a strain on the upper arm put the worker at a disadvantage under most conditions.

This experiment will not always produce the same order of results, especially if it is only a very brief one. Starting differences of dexterity between the operators may outweigh the advantages of any particular arrangement; but it does work well on the whole, and especially when many operators, or long periods of work, are involved the question of the best working plane becomes an important one. The advantage of an inclined plane over the flat surface is that it usually requires fewer head and eye movements.

Positioning is important not only in the lay-out of tools, or in assembly operations, but also in the operation of particular machines, especially when a number of knobs, or switches, or levers, or wheels may have to be manipulated. This is the case, for example, in an engine room, or in a motor car, or in an aircraft cockpit, or in many wireless or radar instruments, and also in a lot of industrial tasks. The more rapid the manipulation required the more important positioning becomes.

Once again the thing to do is not merely to accept what somebody says because he says it, but to find out things for oneself. It is not difficult to construct a light wooden framework on which a number of targets can be mounted in various positions at arm's length from an operator who is seated as depicted in Fig. 12 (opposite page 48). The operator, having been given initial practice with vision, wearing a pair of obscuring goggles, has to try to find the middle of each target in random order and without groping, when appropriate instructions are given to him, using a pencil or a short pointer. Naturally right-handed operators will score better on targets to their right and all subjects on targets immediately in front. There will be little difference between scores outwards to right or left up to about 90 degrees, but beyond that a large increase in difficulty. Targets below shoulder level to an angle of 45 degrees will prove a little easier to find than those exactly at shoulder level, but those above shoulder level at an angle of 45 degrees will be much the hardest. These are the broad results only. Many more details still have to be filled in, and this can be done readily enough by an extension of this experiment. Once again we find that positions above shoulder level are difficult to deal with quickly without error. There are many indications also that controls situated below waist level are especially difficult to find and operate, but this is a matter that needs more experiment.

When two items of control are closely related, so that if one of them has to be used it nearly always happens that the other must be used also, or when an item of control changes an item of display which must now be interpreted, it is very often found that designers have placed the two in very different positions. For example, a control knob on a wireless instrument which is set at waist height operates a display panel which is stuck up above the operator's head. No sensible person would think that experiment was necessary to show that any such arrangement is a thoroughly bad one. But it is strange what can be done when the only questions considered are good looks, or engineering convenience, and many of the questions that have got to be settled about where to place related controls or related items of control and display are not so easy as this one.

2. DIRECTION OF MOVEMENT OF CONTROL

Try the following simple experiment. Mount seven 2-volt lamp bulbs on a block of wood and wire them up to six circular knob switches one immediately below each lamp. Do the same with a second block. The operator is to begin with the left hand lamp lighted, and his job is to switch on each lamp in whatever order he can, and to reach the middle bulb, having lighted each lamp once and none more than once. Make it clear that the correct knob for each move is the one immediately under the light last switched on.

Board one is so wired that a clockwise movement of the first knob lights lamp 7, an anti-clockwise movement of knob 7 lights lamp 2, a clockwise movement of knob 2 lights lamp 6, an anti-clockwise movement of knob 6 lights lamp 3, a clockwise movement of knob 3 lights lamp 5, and an anti-clockwise movement of knob 5 lights lamp 4. Board two is so wired that the movements 1–7, 7–2, 2–6, 6–3 are exactly reversed, but the remaining two movements have the same direction. All wiring is, of course, concealed, and the operator must find the correct directions of control by trial. Take any two operators, explain the problem and its conditions, start them working at the same time, and see who finishes first.

It will be seen that on the one board every direction of movement of control is in that direction towards which the next light will appear. On the second board the first four movements are against this direction and the last two in accord with it.

Many may think that the last two movements on the second board are of the nature of a "catch" and are unfair. But they were put in on purpose, because there are a very large number of machines in common use in which results that are exactly comparable have to be produced sometimes by control movements in one direction and sometimes by movements in another, and often a precisely opposite direction. Tremendous confusion can be caused by this.

For most types of machine-produced change there is some direction of control which is more "natural," or easier to carry out than any other. What these are have to be discovered by experiment, but as soon as the need is realized the experiments are not usually difficult to devise.

3. THE SPEED OF CONTROL MOVEMENTS

Perhaps most people who were asked whether it is easier to make an accurate control movement at high or at low speed would be inclined to prefer the latter. Naturally much depends on the type of movement required, whether, for example, it is a to-and-fro movement or a rotation movement; on the distance of the operating member of the body from its main joint control, whether for example the hand is principally controlled from the wrist, the forearm or the shoulder; and on how many operating main organs of the body have to be brought into play at once, whether for example one hand does the work or two. Also an obviously important consideration is the length of time over which control must be maintained. Speeds that are very good for short bursts of control may have to be somewhat reduced for work which must be continued for, say, longer than about 15 minutes. But in general, and taking all these conditions into account, really slow speed movement is hard to keep up at regular rates, and the most efficient speed for the regulation of accurate controls by the operator is usually a fairly fast one. Speaking very generally, in fact, it is true to say that most human beings can get on better at a rather high speed of working movement, with appropriate short rests, than at a slow rate.

This is very noticeable in rotation movements, which, as everybody knows, are used on a large variety of machines, from common, everyday instances like the bicycle and the sewing machine, to highly technical instruments like those used in tracking the variable course of swift moving targets. Perhaps winding wheels are used mainly because they have a lot of engineering conveniences, and it is certainly high time that more attempts should be made to decide just when and why they are more suitable from the operator's point of view than levers and joy-sticks and push devices of one sort and another. However, with a wheel control requiring hand-wrist movement it will be found that the best winding speed lies within the rate of about 100–200 r.p.m.

The case is not quite so clear as regards to and fro movements, let us say of hand and arm. Some things are definite enough. Such movements are usually smoother, less tiring and more accurate in a horizontal than in a vertical plane, and outwards, away from the middle of the body than inwards. But the question of speed is more complicated. The movement is from rest in one position to rest in another and then back to rest in the first position again, and so on. A limb moving from rest starts relatively slowly, increases its speed and then begins to decrease again in speed short of the end of the movement. When the motion is very rapid these constantly repeated efforts of acceleration and deceleration are apt to become tiring, depending in the main on the distance that has to be travelled. All the same it is very probable that the best speed of to and fro control movements is, for most distances, higher than most people imagine, and that we can say that the human mind and body tolerate high rates of working speed under most conditions which do not require very great mental or muscular effort more easily than they do very slow rates of speed. However, there is need for a lot more experiment about all of this.

4. THE RESISTANCE OF CONTROLS

A very little experimentation will demonstrate that when a control offers practically no resistance at all movements will tend generally, though not always, to be underestimated and so will continue beyond where they are required to go. If on the other hand resistance is great the opposite mistake will often be made. Then when the operator realizes what he is doing he corrects himself too much and falls into reverse error. And so his control is apt to swing from one unsatisfactory extreme to another one.

It seems as if there ought to be some general principles which could be applied to tell us within what limits of resistance any type of machine control should be designed. If there are, they are still waiting to be discovered. A few facts are known which can be expressed in a general way, but many more experiments are needed.

If a control has to be moved from a resting position and requires a fair amount of effort, it is, as a rule, worth going to whatever trouble may be necessary to give the operator mechanical assistance which will come automatically into play at the right moment. Without this he will not only be badly slowed up at the beginning of the movement, but when he does get going, he is likely to move in a jerky and irregular manner, and to get into the bad habit of snatching at the controls.

Machines often have to be operated when a lot of jolting and vibration are present. Maybe the operator is being carried along in the machine, as, for example, if he is driving a heavy type of vehicle. But it makes little difference, whether the jolting directly affects the whole body, as it does in this case, or principally only some part of it, as may well be the case when the machine as a whole is stationary and the vibration is transferred from the control to the limbs that do the operation. Whenever there is a lot of jolting and vibration extremely freely moving controls are usually hard to handle accurately. Under bumpy conditions, if a lever, or joy-stick type of control is being used, requiring to and fro movements of hand and arm, accuracy is usually improved by a frictional resistance at the handle of about 2 lb.

Even if there is no jolting it seems that a type of friction which automatically increases with the velocity of movement tends to increase the accuracy of continuous winding, but not of to and fro movements.

The explanation of these tendencies is as yet far from clear. Moreover, much depends upon the rates of speed of the control movements. When the adjustment must be both slow and regular, increase of resistance above a small amount is likely to lead to trouble.

5. A DEMONSTRATION

Let us see if we can build two simple machines which will show us these principles in operation. That will be the best way, perhaps indeed the only way, by which we can convince ourselves and other people how important they are. It is not at all difficult to do this in a number of different ways and here is one that will certainly work.

Look at Fig. 13 (opposite page 49), which shows us the two instruments, alike in what they do, but different in the ways they do it. A light aluminium indicator, seen immediately on the right of each dial face is driven by a mains motor and revolves at a constant speed. This in turn sets the "error dial hand" in motion. When the indicator is being driven without interruption the readings on both dial faces will be exactly alike. At the rear of each instrument is a small winding handle of $1\frac{1}{2}$ inches radius, which is a suitable size for any regular winding movement requiring only moderate effort from the operator. The handle is so connected with the driving mechanism of the aluminium indicator that if the operator contrives to rotate it at the correct speed and in the required direction the indicator will be stationary all the time, that is to say, the operator is attempting exactly to counteract the motor produced movement.

Now consider the principal differences between the two instruments. On the one the winding handle is set at just about waist height, and on the other at over shoulder height. On the one the gear relation, from winding handle to indicator, is such that the operator must keep to a speed of 100 r.p.m., and on the other so that he must, for perfect winding, go at the far slower rate of 14 r.p.m.

On both settings the operator must wind smoothly in a clockwise direction and at a constant speed. Provided the correct speed is maintained the indicator will remain motionless, as already stated, and the "error dial hand" will not be changing its position. This hand records any difference between the actual winding rate and the speed of the motor, and errors accumulate on the dial concerned whenever the operator is winding too fast or too slowly. On one machine, if the operator is winding too slowly, the indicator will rotate in an anti-clockwise direction, and if too fast in a clockwise direction. The operator must then correct the anti-clockwise rotation of the indicator by speeding up the clockwise winding of the handwheel, or the clockwise rotation of the indicator by a slower movement of the handwheel in the same direction. In the case of the other machine the indication of error and the corrective movement are reversed in direction, so that an anti-clockwise movement of the indicator is the signal to the operator to slow down and a clockwise movement to

Fig. 11.

Fig. 12.

Fig. 13.

speed up. A normal operator will find the first type of winding correction the "natural" one, and the second "unnatural" and difficult.

Any two operators of comparable height can be chosen at random. Give them a brief trial run to get them used to the "feel" of the handle. Then start them going simultaneously. In a short trial of two or three minutes it will usually be found that the dial recorder on the badly designed instrument has moved completely round the dial face while the one on the well designed instrument has moved not more than 5 to 10 units. In every case there will be a very marked difference in favour of the good design. If the operators are changed over, the "good" one will now become the "bad" one.

The experiment can be made more impressive still if the indicator is made to revolve at a varying speed in a way that the operator cannot foresee.

With a constant speed revolution of the indicator it may be found that after a fairly short practice period of five or ten minutes the operators are coming more closely together and at length each may be doing as well as the other. But go on with the experiment and before very long they will differ again, one from the other, and always it is the machine more than the operator that makes the difference, for now the bad features begin to produce fatigue.

6. GETTING TIRED

Everybody knows that if we have a long continued spell of activity we tend to get tired, whether at work or at play, and to do less well than we did at the beginning. There are certainly two and probably three kinds of fatigue; fatigue of muscles; fatigue in skilled work; and fatigue which is really an expression of a strong desire to go to sleep.

If particular groups of muscles have to perform a lot of

hard work they get fatigued, and very little can be done about it except to give the muscles a properly timed period of rest. A considerable amount is known about muscular fatigue, but we are more interested just now in discovering what happens to people who have to try to keep up a skilled activity for a long period, no part of which involves very heavy physical effort which has to be exactly repeated time after time. For it is skill rather than a great amount of effort that is required in the majority of machine operations.

Let us begin, however, by considering not a machine-controlled operation, but one with which everybody is familiar—reading. First get somebody to sit facing a good strong light, ask him to read a few lines of print from a book or newspaper, and watch his eyes. You will see that his eyes do not move evenly and regularly along the line of the print. They move in jerks, very rapidly, sometimes glancing back for a moment; and then, usually, in a single sweep from near the end of one line to near the beginning of the next. The movements are so rapid that nothing can be seen clearly while they are being made, and the reading is actually done while the eyes are at rest, between each pair of movements. These rests, or "fixation pauses" as they are usually called, are short. They last about two-fifths of a second in the case of young children, but drop, by about the age of ten years, to something near a quarter of a second. Ninety per cent or more of the total time taken in reading is spent in actually seeing the material and only 10 per cent or less in making the movements, once reading has become a skilled operation. Obviously the eye movements and pauses of a good reader must be controlled and timed with astonishing accuracy.

Many experiments have been carried out to discover when people get tired as a result of long-continued reading, and what happens if they do. By far the most extensive and carefully designed of these are the studies made by Dr. Leonard Carmichael and Professor W. F. Dearborn in America.[1] These experimenters provided the best possible reading conditions, with good ventilation, heating and with good light, a comfortable position, and clear print or microfilm, and they set their readers, who were college and high school students, to read without a break first for two hours, and later for six.

In the first, the two-hour, experiment there was no check on how well the readers understood their material. In the second, or six-hour experiment, what were called "comprehension" tests were introduced every twenty-five minutes and at the end of the experiment. These tests did not interrupt the work, for they consisted of questions which had to be read, and could be marked very simply by the readers. They were a check, both for the experimenters and for the readers, of how well the latter were getting on, and whether they were keeping up their initial standard.

All eye movements and fixation pauses were exactly and automatically recorded.

The two-hour reading spells seemed quite definitely to be producing tiredness, or fatigue. Towards the end readers would often stop for a few seconds, or their eyes would wander over the lines of print and apparently see nothing, certainly read nothing. Sentences and even paragraphs would be left out, and lines of print be missed. It seemed certain that the muscles which bring about eye movements were getting tired, and working irregularly.

At this stage the "comprehension" tests were introduced, and at once the whole picture changed. Now, every twenty-five minutes, the reader could check up how well he was doing his job. In six hours there were no signs of any increasing failure, no skipping, no aimless wandering

[1] For the full story see *Reading and Visual Fatigue*, by L. Carmichael and W. F. Dearborn, Houghton Mifflin Co., 1947.

of the eyes over the lines of print, no increase of errors, and no breakdown in the pattern of regularly controlled eye movements and pauses.

One curious thing about fatigue is that its action is very often delayed. Nothing noticeable happens while the tiring activity is going on, but later, sometimes a good many hours later, odd mistakes get made when something else is being done.

But in this case, although the experimenters looked for it, they found no "hidden fatigue," no delayed effects.

Now it may seem as if this is a very special instance. For one thing the muscles that move the eyes are large and strong, considering the work they have to do; and they get a rest between every pair of movements.

But there are other experiments, involving much more varied muscle play, which seem to illustrate exactly the same principle. During the war many people became interested in pilot fatigue. The aircraft pilot, flying by means of his instruments, has to use his eyes, his hands, his legs and feet and other parts of his body to make a long series of accurate and well-timed movements. Except in unusual circumstances the physical effort is not great, but a high level of skill must be maintained. It seemed certain that when the pilot had to make a very long flight of several hours his skill suffered. Movements were not properly timed and so interfered one with another. Signals for movement were not responded to, or were responded to only after they had become much greater than they needed to be at the beginning.

We found out that all these things and several more did in fact happen when we built an experimental cockpit at Cambridge, with a complete recording equipment which gave us an exact picture of what the pilot was doing. He could sit in the cockpit and take it off for as long a flight as was desired, flying all the time on his instruments, and being given navigational instructions exactly as he might have been if he had been really airborne. The whole experimental flight was divided into spells, each of a quarter of an hour. A clock was there for the pilot and if he remembered to look at it at the end of each fifteen minutes he could use it as a check to tell him if he was working accurately and with perfect timing, and doing what was required without hurry and without delay. Sometimes this possible check was ignored and then, especially after about two hours or so, the pilot's skill would usually begin to break up. But provided the check was used and if the pilot was keen, physically fit, and skilled, he could continue for very long periods indeed without any fall in the level of his performance. One pilot, for example, continued without a break for twelve hours, being fed while he worked, and remained as good at the end as he was at the beginning. And in this case too, although we looked for it, we could find no evidence for "delayed fatigue."

The case is not yet proved—perhaps somebody who reads this will plan the investigation which will discover the exact truth—but it is not at all unlikely that provided the equipment and conditions of activity are designed and controlled with a view to what the senses, the muscles and the mind have been developed to do well; provided worry and anxiety can be avoided, and provided no great and continued physical effort is involved, any fit human being can go on working for a very long time indeed without fatigue. Perhaps he can go on right up to the time at which he begins to fail because he must needs go to sleep.

Among all these conditions which must be attended to if unnecessary fatigue is to be avoided, the most interesting is the one that we have just been considering. For it shows that the mind has a direct part to play in influencing the ways in which the various mechanisms of the body do their work. The man who knows how he is getting on can go on longer. Later we shall see also that "knowledge of results," or "knowledge of achievement" may help anybody who sets out to do new things to learn them quickly and well.

8. FATIGUE IN THE CASE OF SKILL

Although skill which does not demand difficult muscular effort can be kept up without fatigue for much longer periods than most people think, provided the conditions under which it is exercised can be arranged to fit in with what the body and mind are naturally able to do well, we must not suppose that fatigue of this kind need not occur under any conditions. Poor ventilation, or lighting; uncomfortable postures or movements; excess of heat or cold; speed and the number of things that have to be attended to at the same time, or in rapid succession, and many other conditions belonging to the work or play environment, will most surely lead to fatigue if they are not carefully controlled. So will many drugs. So will lack of sleep. And probably most important of all, so will the accumulation of small worries and anxieties.

This is true whether the skill is what is called mental, or physical, or a combination of both. Worry or anxiety for example is probably more responsible than anything else for the fact that many people who are working for critical examinations get extremely tired and, as we say, "lose their grip." And it is also one of the main reasons why the so-called dangerous occupations and sports are the ones in which fatigue is most noticeable and troublesome.

It is therefore important as well as interesting to know what is likely to happen to skill when people begin to get tired. The main effects can be stated very briefly.

The first thing to suffer is timing. This gets ragged. Some parts of the skill are hurried, other parts delayed. In general it is more common to find the right thing done at the wrong moment than to find an entirely wrong thing done. A special case of this is that when the operator has to notice a changing signal, he will often do nothing until a much bigger change has taken place than was necessary at the beginning. It seems as if the operator's senses have become less acute, so that they are no longer able to detect a difference which before was appreciated without difficulty. But this need not be the case at all. For if the operator is now given a special test it is usually found that his senses are able to make just as delicate and exact discriminations as they were at the beginning. What happens is that there has to be a bigger change before he considers that it is worth while doing anything about it. The danger is that in most cases he does not know that he is waiting until the change is becoming really critical, but thinks he is working or playing as well as ever.

Another important thing is that in many forms of skill there are actions which do not have to be regularly repeated but must be done every now and then, and there are signals which do not lie right in those parts of the field of attention that are prominent, but are on the edges of the display. When a performer begins to get tired these occasional actions and distant signals are very likely to go forgotten or unnoticed.

Finally, as fatigue increases, the operator usually becomes more and more conscious of sensations that seem to be coming from his own body. He grumbles about aches and pains, and the more the state of his own body attracts his attention the less able he is to give proper consideration to the correct distribution and timing of his movements in response to the signals that come to him from his environment.

When anybody reaches a fairly advanced stage of fatigue he usually knows perfectly well that he is tired. He may then make a special effort and pull himself through. Or he may go along very cautiously and avoid bad errors. Or he may, if he can, give himself a rest. The dangerous stage is generally the early one. For then the operator often does not recognize that he is getting tired and he is not on his guard against mistakes. Because he does not time his movements smoothly and well he must often do more work to produce the same results, and so fatigue goes on piling up at an increasing rate. This is what makes it particularly important to know something about what happens to skill as fatigue comes on; for then we can take a short rest, if that is possible, or at least proceed with greater care and caution.

9. CONCLUSIONS

1. A lot of people spend a lot of time nowadays in operating machines. To do this they must interpret signals and adjust controls, and both controls and signals should be designed to fit what most operators can do best.

2. Tools and materials for work ought not to be allowed to lie about "all over the place." A simple experiment can settle their best working positions.

3. Speaking generally the best working surface is an inclined plane. Vertical panels are usually bad.

4. Machine controls which have to be found quickly and operated regularly should be placed below shoulder height and not much below waist height.

5. The direction of movement of a control may be "natural" or "unnatural" and experiment must be used to decide which is which. In general if a change of direction of a control is used to produce a change of direction in a display, the two directions should be made to match as nearly as possible.

6. Most people can speed up their movements without loss of regularity, over fairly wide limits, more easily than they can slow them down. For all bodily movements there is a range of speed which is the best. In the case of

regular winding movements it is best, if possible, to use a radius of winding handle of 2 to 3 inches, and a speed of 100 to 200 r.p.m.

7. If machines have to be operated under bumpy conditions controls should be given greater resistance than if the operational conditions are perfectly stable.

8. When people go on doing the same things, or nearly the same things for a long time they very often begin to lose their efficiency, and we have to distinguish three sorts of cases: (*a*) when heavy muscular work is being done, (*b*) when there is little muscular effort but a lot of skill, (*c*) when there is need for sleep.

In (*a*) the muscles cannot go on making all the effort that is required and must be given a rest; in (*b*) the different parts of the skill cease to fit well together and the movements become wrongly timed; in (*c*) the whole work tends to go by fits and starts.

There is evidence that when skill has to be kept up for a long time, if the performer is given a way in which he can check his performance from time to time and satisfy himself that he is keeping up the standard with which he started, his bodily mechanism can go on working just as well as ever for very long times indeed.

CHAPTER THREE

The Mind Observes

So far we have been concerned principally with ways in which the mind helps the special senses and the muscles of the body to do their work. We must now turn to some of the things which everybody considers to be more especially the jobs of the mind itself. The proper thing to begin with is observation, or, as the psychologist prefers to call it, perception; for it is through some form or another of this that we learn whatever we know about the world in which we live, and the information that we gain in this way we use in the attempt to solve whatever problems we meet at home, or at school, in work, or in play.

Of course it is true that in order to observe anything at all we must use our special senses, and very often more than one of them: vision, hearing, the various forms of touch and temperature, the sense of movement and vibration, smell and taste. But everybody very soon finds that we can look at things and not see them, hear sounds but not listen to them, make movements and not know that we have made them. Observation is a lot more than just using the special senses, and the part of it that has to do with picking out some things and ignoring others, with putting a meaning on the things that are picked out, and with connecting the different things that are selected in various ways, is the part that we all agree to be the special business of the mind.

Clearly the senses do not all work in the same ways. Touch and hearing work more quickly than seeing, and seeing a lot more quickly than smell and taste and particularly than the sense of pain. In hearing the material has to be stretched out in a line, one item following another, but in seeing quite a lot of items can be all present and all dealt with together. Among the senses the one that is most frequently used by human beings, the one that is generally preferred above all others, and the one that is able to deal with the greatest variation of conditions is sight, and so most of the cases that we shall be studying in our experiments will be concerned with vision.

1. HOW MANY THINGS CAN BE OBSERVED "ALL AT ONCE"

Very often it is interesting, and it may be important, to know how many objects of a particular kind are present to observation all at once, or in extremely quick succession. If there is time and opportunity to count them, of course, we can quickly deal with large numbers. But what if there is not?

Long ago psychologists devised an experiment which they called measuring the "span of apprehension," to settle this question. Get six blank postcards and mark them with small dots of ink in a completely haphazard arrangement in numbers from 4 to 9. Get your observer to sit in a good light, which must remain the same all the time and to look in the right direction. Then expose each card in turn, seeing that the order of cards does not follow a regular order of number of dots, every card for less than one quarter of a second, but every card as nearly as possible for the same length of time. As soon as a card is withdrawn the observer writes or speaks the number of dots which he thinks he saw. Repeat the whole series three or four times, each time with the cards in a different random order.

You will find that most observers can report accurately up to five to seven dots, but that beyond this number many mistakes will be made. If you use lines, or small squares, or words, or even figures that contain quite a lot of detail, so long as the complete items can be treated as units, the limits of immediate numerical observation will be the same.

Suppose instead of having everything all there at once we try things that follow one another quickly. Get a metronome and arrange the successive beats to come at intervals of a quarter of a second or less. The observer must try not to count. You will find that most people can accurately distinguish groups of beats up to about eight, and then they will break down.

Naturally if the dots, or other visual shapes, or if the beats, are definitely arranged into groups, the number that can be accurately reported without counting is much higher. However, it is clear that the limits to the correct observation of numbers, apart from counting, are narrow and sharp.

2. CAN SOME PARTS OF OBJECTS BE MORE EASILY OBSERVED THAN OTHERS?

A much more interesting question is whether there are some parts, or characteristics, of objects that can be observed more easily or that make a stronger impression, than others. Try to read paragraph A and paragraph B below and take the time from start to finish.

A.

When any practised reader runs his eyes rapidly along the lines of print, is it true to say that all parts of the letters or words read are equally important, or are there perhaps some parts which make a stronger impression than others? Most readers would probably be inclined to say that all parts of the shapes which they interpret have about the same influence.

B.

But here is an experiment which may show that he is wrong. For it usually takes longer to read words when only the bottom halves of the letters are seen than it does to read the same number of words when only the top halves are represented. In fact the upper halves of letters make more impression, or carry more meaning than their bottom halves.

In the case of the letters of the alphabet, no doubt the superior importance of the upper halves is partly due to the shapes themselves, for if we take the ordinary Roman form, for every letter that projects below the line, about seven project above the line. But apart altogether from that, people of all races and types of training do in fact pay more attention to the upper parts of nearly all kinds of visual display. Graphical records for example can just as well be built below as above a base line, or on a descending as compared with ascending plot. More people will prefer the latter and will read them more quickly and correctly.

Here is another interesting thing about reading and horizontal visual displays generally. If you take any eight letters which do not make a sensible word and arrange for a reader to be looking at a spot exactly in between where the fourth and fifth letters will come, and if you then let the reader see the eight letters for not more than a quarter of a second, you can discover which letters will be most correctly reported. They will not be the ones in the immediate neighbourhood of his fixation point. The first two letters are nearly three times more likely to be observed correctly than the fourth or fifth, and the last one more than twice as likely.

Now try to read paragraphs C and D, timing the task as before:

To split words in half makes reading far more difficult

C.

. I fa th begin ar th en o wo ar the mo impo pa ar th begin ma a gre impre ar ca mo mea th th en Bu fir ar la hal c wo ar bo mo diffi t re th upp ar low hal ar ea c the tw parag w prob b fou to ta lon t re th th oth

D.

lled ıd tised lers ın ad ı st ıf ty :ers ıged n :ical mns ı ›ut een- ıd-ı- ılf ›nds. ıey ın so ad ty ur- ter rds n st ·er ıteen ›nds ıd ty ;ht- ter rds n ›ut teen- ıd-ı- ılf ›nds. t ms at ›t ll :ers, ıd ›t ll f ›ry ›rd ·ed e ad.

(For a full transcription of these passages see p. 76.)

than to use only the upper or lower parts of the letters, keeping the words complete. At the same time most people can make a reasonably good shot at the sense if first halves only are given, while when last halves stand alone reading becomes very difficult and sometimes impossible. If you like to try, it is of course easy enough to prepare a piece of writing in which only the middle halves of words are given. Reading then becomes merely guess-work, and hard guess-work at that.

The same kinds of things are true of any sort of visual observation. Some things stand out much more clearly than others. Very often our particular interests have a lot to do with the matter; but apart altogether from that, the place of objects makes a difference to accurate observation. And in vision objects that appear in the upper part of the field and towards the left are more likely to be correctly reported than those that appear towards the right.

3. SIMILARITY AND DISSIMILARITY

Still more important than all this are the ways in which people are able to spot things that are alike and things that are different.

Write down on a blank card ten or fifteen letters of the alphabet in haphazard order and position, and put one number somewhere amongst them. If you show the card for a single brief glance to a lot of people and ask them what it contained you will find the number reported more often than it ought to be if it had just the same chance of being observed as any other single item in the same position. The same sort of thing will happen if you draw a lot of small closed figures in straight lines and put in one with a curved boundary. There are plenty of everyday observations which illustrate the same fact. For example, a single shot in a cinema film, the incidents of which do not fit very well with the general run of the picture, is pretty sure to make a marked impression on the observer.

Look at the two lines of figures that follow (Fig. 14)

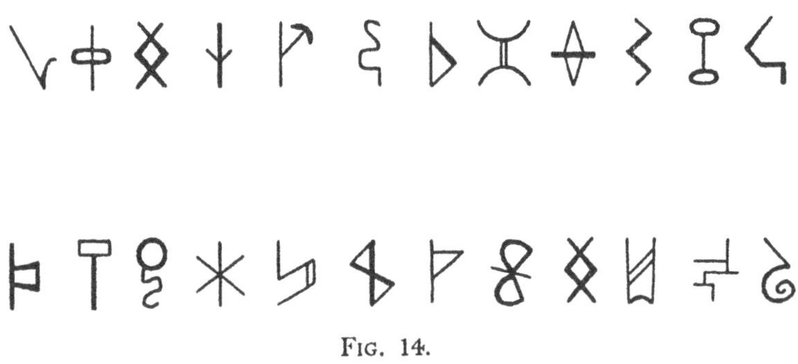

FIG. 14.

and write down any one thing, and not more than one thing, about them that you consider to be of particular interest.

Now do exactly the same with the next two lines of figures (Fig. 15) and be careful not to go on reading the

FIG. 15.

following text until you have completed the task.

The record that is required is that the first pair agree in one item only and the second pair differ in one item only. The better experiment is to copy these designs and give them to other people to observe, without making any preliminary remarks about similarity or difference, for such remarks may of course be used as a cue to what is wanted.

We did exactly this experiment in one of the lectures at the Royal Institution, using lantern slides and giving everybody plenty of time to make their observation. Results were sent in by 195 members of the audience. Of these eleven noticed the single point of difference and only four the single point of agreement. In addition forty-six observers were on the right lines as regards the difference, but did not exactly identify the items concerned, but this was true of seven only in the case of the agreement.

Any ingenious person can easily vary this experiment in a number of ways. The items can be changed, their arrangement or disposition can be according to any kind of pattern desired, and the number of points of agreement and disagreement can be different. But within wide limits the same thing is true: it is easier to notice that two situations are different than to detect that they are alike;

easier to observe the points or principles as to which they differ than to notice the points or principles as to which they agree. Later on we shall find how this extremely simple fact about observation carries with it a lot of important results for behaviour and for thinking. (See pp. 115–19).

4. RAPID OBSERVATION

Generally in everyday life nobody has much time to observe things in great detail. We rush along a road at high speed in a motor-car, or through the countryside in an express train. The eyes can rest on nothing for long. Nevertheless, if we have to, we can say quite a lot about what we believe we have seen, and, though not all of it is always correct, a good deal of it is. Or think of what happens in play, especially in a quick ball game. It is astonishing how often the good player will make the correct response when it can be proved beyond doubt that he cannot possibly have observed more than a very small part of the things that are prompting him. Clearly enough, not a little of what is usually called observation is really something else, but we shall come upon this again later. Let us consider now what happens when observations follow one another in rapid succession, and something must be done about each one of them as it occurs.

Already we have seen how, in cases of this sort, anticipation can come to our help (see pp. 31–3), but let us look at the matter a little more closely, for there are some things about it that are still not well understood.

Many experimenters have shown that in rapid reading, the interpretation of one line of print is normally very much influenced both by the preceding and by the succeeding line. There is, that is to say, some way in which interpretation runs ahead of the point that has been actually reached. A particular case of this is the way in which rapid blind readers sometimes deal with their raised type (braille).

"One girl who reads with an unusually high degree of accuracy, speed, and comprehension, vowed that she could not possibly read ahead with one finger because her mind could not carry two sets of ideas at the same time. A little later, when this girl was asked to read some fairly difficult material, she was discovered reading so far ahead on the next line with her left hand that her two forefingers met in the middle of each line." This kind of observation has been many times repeated. The distance ahead at which the rapid blind reader is working may vary from a few letters to three or four words.

There is one particularly interesting experiment which anybody can develop considerably for himself. Make a two-way east-west switch and get a number of people to operate it freely as rapidly as they can. It will be found that most persons can make the required successive contacts about twelve times a second. Now take a sheet of cardboard 8 inches by 10 inches and draw 30 circles of 1-inch diameter arranging them in horizontal lines six in each line. Inside each circle draw a pointer, radiating from the centre and terminating near the circumference in an arrow head, the pointers to be arranged east or west in irregular order. Let the same people read the directions of each pointer starting from top left as fast as he can, either as "east" "west" or as "right" "left," as he prefers. You will find that this takes about 19 seconds. Finally, let your operators use the switch to indicate the direction of the pointers, with the same order of reading as before, and again working as fast as possible. It would perhaps be expected that the time required for this would be something near the sum of the two times for free movement and reading, possibly a little more than this, since now the movement is not just a regular east-west succession. In fact, it will be found that the time for reading *plus* manipulation is about 19½ seconds or less. The order of trials can be varied so as to make sure that the reduction of reading or of manipulation time is not merely due to practice. It looks as if when we have to work at high speed, combining the interpretation of successive signals with movements made in response to the signals, something in the performance becomes easier. Exactly how this effect is produced nobody knows, but probably it is one of the cases in which observation runs a little ahead of performance and speeds up the action when the moment of the latter is reached. Maybe this has a lot to do with the fact that in everyday life quite complicated skills can be successfully carried out at high speed, though there are also other things as well that help to make this possible. In one way and another it is pretty clear that in rapid observation the mind tends to push on ahead of the body.

5. THE PERCEPTUAL SETTING

Partly, no doubt, because most of our everyday observation has to be completed quickly, but also because the visual mechanism is built to take in a lot of things all at once, whenever we can, we observe things as a whole, giving them a single name, or a short, descriptive label. Only when there is such a lot of detail that it cannot easily be combined into a single object or situation; or as a result of specialized training in the observation of detail, do we go over the material with which we have to deal systematically, concentrating first on one bit and then on another. So it comes about that the setting, or background, of objects that are presented to us has a great influence upon what we observe, and the same physical objects can be interpreted differently if their setting is changed.

Look, for example, at the next picture (Fig. 16). It

FIG. 16.

will probably be seen as a not particularly brilliant drawing of an oak tree in leaf, standing on a mound with a good deal of rather scrubby undergrowth.

As a matter of fact this was a popular picture in England in 1815, after the Battle of Waterloo. It was published with the following inscription:

THE ROYAL ALLIED OAK AND SELF-CREATED MUSHROOM KINGS

Behold the Oak, whose firm fix'd stay,
  Doth check Oppression's course,
Whose slightest branch can ne'er decay,
  While strong with Virtue's force.

Our much-loved Sovereign decks the branch,
  The highest of the Tree;
And peaceful Louis tho' driven from France,
  Among its boughs you'll see.

The Regent's Portrait next behold,
  Whose councils Wisdom guides;
And Russia's noble Monarch bold
  Who checked the Tyrant's strides.

Immortal Wellington next is seen,
  Whose fame can ne'er expire;
And veteran Blucher's warlike mien,
  That kindled Napoleon's ire.

The Mushroom Race you have to seek
  In weeds about the Root,
Who scarce dare at the Oak to peep
  Or at its Princely fruit.

1815.

If you now go back to the picture you will be able to see clearly the faces in the branches, though you may still have a bit of a hunt for those in the undergrowth. At once an interesting question is likely to crop up. When you see the faces clearly what happens to the tree? It certainly does not disappear, but it seems to slide into the background, almost as if it need not be a tree at all. Sometimes when we observe a thing in one way we do not, and perhaps cannot, observe it another way at the same time, and sometimes all that happens is that one way stands out, but the other way is there all the same.

Which happens seems to depend largely upon how the

setting is fixed for us. When it is principally made by a mass of details, all present together at the time of the observation, as in this case of the tree, for example, it is more likely that the second thing will happen. But here is another experiment.

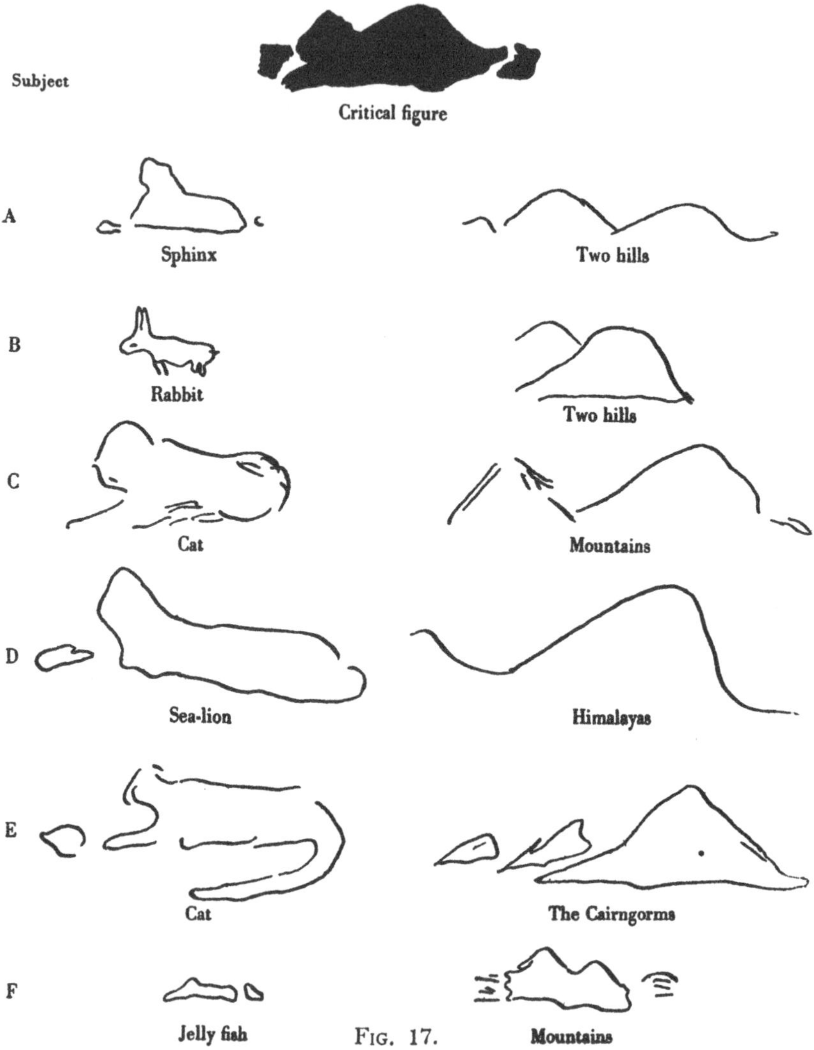

FIG. 17.

Take the black silhouette at the top of Fig. 17 and arrange for a number of people to be able to see it for a brief glance of half a second or less. Before you show it say, "I am going to show you a black silhouette figure. It may not seem to you to represent anything very definitely, but it could quite well stand for animals of some sort." Ask your observers to describe, or, better still, to draw, what they have seen. Next show exactly the same shape to other people under the same conditions, but the instructions will now run, "I am going to show you a black silhouette figure. It may not seem to you to represent anything very definitely, but it could quite well stand for a landscape with mountains or hills." In Fig. 17 all the drawings on the left are selected from reproductions made by observers who had the first instructions, and all those on the right from attempts made after the second instructions. It is usually not difficult to get an observer who has seen the shapes one way to see them the other way, but very hard to get anybody to see them both ways at once. Here the setting is given by instructions which cover the whole of whatever has to be perceived.

There is a third way in which the material of observation can be given its setting, and this is one from which in fact nobody can ever really escape. Everybody brings to the task of observing an amount of information, or knowledge, which has already been acquired. Take a glance at Fig. 18, for example, and then try to describe it.

FIG. 18.

Actually this is a bit of American-Indian picture writing. What it indicates is, "an old woman, a descendant of an ancient tribal name 'Owl,' bought on credit one plug of smoking tobacco of oblong shape, like the usual packages of such material. Also she bought two quarts of kerosene oil. The price was twenty cents. The account was settled by the barter of a basket." But, of course, nobody except an Indian belonging to the tribe concerned, at the time concerned—which was towards the end of the nineteenth century—or a white settler who lived in the same neighbourhood would be in the least likely to see anything of the kind in this odd collection of drawings.

Here it is very likely that doubts may begin to creep in. It may seem as if all this talk about settings may have a lot to do with interpretation, but not much with observation proper. The setting may make us observe this or that part of the detail, and interpret it in a particular way. But surely, it may be said, provided an observer has normal senses, and a mind that is not all odd and twisty, what he really observes, when he is attending to the same details, must be exactly the same as what any other comparable person observes. Perhaps if we drop out everything possible in the way of setting we shall get nearer to something that can be called "pure observation." Let us try to do this and see what happens.

6. OBSERVATION WITHOUT A SETTING

Strictly speaking, there is no observation without a setting. In the first place all observation consists in distinguishing something from something else. Even if we take a sheet of white paper and draw an oblique black mark on it we can see the black mark as a line on a white ground, or, with a little effort, we can see a white sheet with a slit in it, through which a line of black background appears. If we call whatever is distinguished the "figure" and whatever it is distinguished from, the "ground," we shall find that the qualities of what is observed differ according to its treatment as figure or as ground. Many psychologists have attempted to work out what these qualities are, but this is a complicated topic, still, in many ways, a matter for dispute, and we need not consider it here.

There is another kind of setting from which we cannot escape. This is whatever we may bring with us when we observe which comes from our general education and training. But provided we keep to observers whose chances in these respects have been pretty much the same, and we keep off highly specialized material, we can be reasonably certain that the effects of education and training will be sufficiently equalized.

Then we certainly do find that if we use material of rather simple structure, so that all its parts can be appreciated at once, within the same social group, observation becomes both more definite and more exactly the same. Take these two figures, for example:

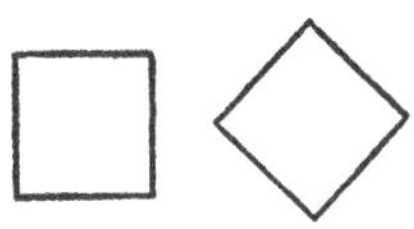

As soon as we see them we probably find ourselves saying of the first "square" and of the second "diamond." We do not confuse them, or see them as the same figures tilted round a bit and set on different bases. Each is perfectly stable and is sharply distinguished from the other, though it could be treated as the other in a different position. When we change the square into this 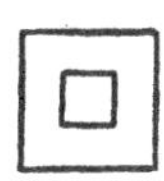 the facts are not quite so clear. For at once we can, and if we go on looking at it without any particular instructions we probably shall, see it as (*a*) a small square inside a larger one; (*b*) a larger square enclosing a smaller one; (*c*) a picture frame with broad edges;

(*d*) a small square *in front of* a larger one, or (*e*) a small square behind a larger one. And if we draw it like this

(*a*) and (*b*) will almost certainly drop out; (*c*) almost certainly will disappear, and we shall seem bound to see it as a solid object, something like a lampshade. As we go on looking at it we shall see, maybe, the small end nearer to us, and then suddenly the whole thing will reverse, and the small end appears farther away, only to change again the next moment or so.

If we like to experiment with almost any simple closed figures we shall find the same kind of thing happening. The simple figure without a special setting is seen in the same way by all comparable observers. We add a few lines and at once it loses its quality of definiteness and becomes now one form and now another. Now we add a few more lines and again we all observe it in the same ways. But not in one way only; it jigs about from one way to another and back again. It has become a true "reversible figure." We shall have to study more carefully these shapes that have the same limited number of ways of appearing to all of us, but which can move rapidly or slowly from one way to another as we go on attending to them. They are particularly interesting, and so far as we have got as yet, it is reasonable to suppose that their changes must be in some way connected with the absence of any specific setting.

Meanwhile let us have one more illustration which will show us that with a little ingenuity it is possible to construct a "reversible figure" which contains a considerable amount of detail.

If you look at Fig. 19 you can perhaps see a rather charming young lady, with her face turned away over her right shoulder. You can detect just the tip of a nose, and above it an eyelash and a black circlet round her neck.

FIG. 19.

But go on looking and it will change into a face of an old woman in full profile. The cheek bone and the chin become a large hooked nose, the ear an eye, the black neck band a very sharp mouth, and below the mouth is an upturned chin. As you look the picture changes from one to the other; but it is never more than one at a time.

7. CONCLUSIONS

1. The number of items that most people can visually observe in a single glance is 5 to 7, and this number is more or less independent of the amount of detail contained in any single item.

2. The upper parts and the left-hand portions of a visual field are on the whole the easiest to observe, and anything contained in them on the whole the most accurately reported.

3. Single differences among a lot of similarities are easier to observe than single similarities among a lot of differences, and in general the differences between one situa-

tion and another are more striking than their likenesses.

4. In rapid observation as a rule the senses run ahead of the mind and items are observed some time before they may be interpreted, and especially before any actions based upon the interpretations are carried out.

5. Observation depends to a very great extent on the setting that is provided, so that exactly the same forms may be seen or not seen, interpreted in one way or in another according to their framework or background. This framework may be constituted by accompanying detail, by particular instructions given to the observer, or by information that is not expressed at all but is brought by the observer to his task.

6. When there is no very definite setting it often happens that objects are seen first with one shape or meaning and then with another. These "reversible figures" as they are called raise some very interesting questions and must be further studied.

[*Correction of paragraphs A, B, C, D, on pp. 60–62*]

A.

When any practised reader runs his eyes rapidly along the lines of print, is it true to say that all parts of the letters or words are equally important, or are there perhaps some parts which make a stronger impression than others? Most readers would probably be inclined to say that all parts of the shapes which they interpret have about the same influence.

B.

But here is an experiment which may show that he is wrong. For it usually takes longer to read words when only the bottom halves of the letters are seen than it does to read the same number of words when only the top halves are represented. In fact the upper halves of letters make more impression, or carry more meaning than their bottom halves.

C.

In fact the beginnings and the ends of words are their most important parts, and the beginnings make a greater impression and carry more meaning that the ends. but first and last halves of words are both more difficult to read than upper and lower halves, and each of these two paragraphs will probably be found to take longer to read than the others.

D.

Skilled and practised readers can read a list of fifty letters arranged in vertical columns in about fifteen-and-a-half seconds. They can also read fifty four-letter words in just over seventeen seconds and fifty eight-letter words in about nineteen-and-a-half seconds. It seems that not all letters, and not all of every word need be read.

CHAPTER FOUR

The Mind connects one thing with others

When we experiment on observation in a laboratory we can select an object which is not regarded as connected with anything else that is present at the same time, or that was present not long before. We can show this object to an observer under carefully controlled conditions, and try to find out exactly how it is interpreted and described. The object is then often treated as detached from any others; and the observation considered as complete in itself and not as forming one member of a connected chain of observations, though the latter is generally what happens when we observe anything in everyday life.

Our previous chapter showed us, however, that if we do literally treat the object and its observation in this isolated way, we to some extent deceive ourselves. For whether in the laboratory or outside of it nothing ever is observed except in a setting of past experience and present interests. We may, as we then saw, try to make these as nearly as possible the same for everybody, and when we do this, the natural procedure seems to be to use objects whose structure is as simple as possible and to remove any very definite frame or setting. Then we may easily run up against the curious case in which what is perceived appears to alternate from one shape, or meaning, to another.

Outside, in the street, on the playing-field, in school, or in the factory, hardly anything that we notice seems to have that kind of reversibility, except, perhaps, the cases in which contrasting movements are involved. We surely, then, ought to be able to find ways of making these "reversible figures" more stable, so that one interpretation ceases to pass into another, or at any rate does so less rapidly.

1. MORE ABOUT REVERSIBLE FIGURES

Let us take one of the most familiar of these simple figures, the reversible cross (Fig. 20).

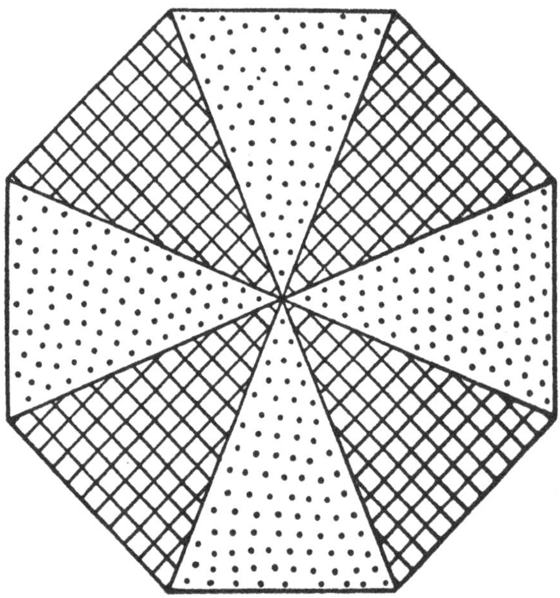

Fig. 20.

If you look steadily at the middle of this design you will see either a + or a × cross standing out, almost as if it were in front of the other. Continue to look without changing the point of fixation, and soon, all of a sudden, the cross that was prominent at first will recede into the background and the other will stand out. The two crosses will then go on reversing at fairly rapid intervals. To some degree you can successfully decide when you will see one and when another, and so speed up or slow down the rate of reversal. But it is not possible, by an effort of will, to prevent any change from happening.

Now if, instead of gazing at the middle point of the figure, you put a prominent mark on one of the arms of one of the crosses, well away from the middle, and look at that, you will find that the cross which carries the mark

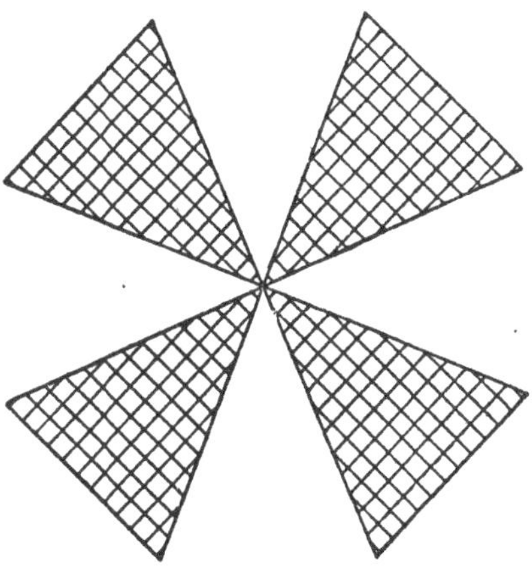

FIG. 21.

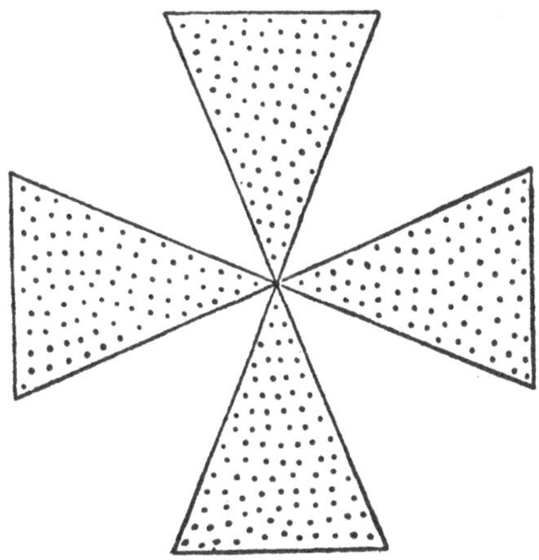

FIG. 22.

tends to become a little more stable. But still reversals occur. Much the same result follows if one of the crosses is filled in in some very bright colour and the other left dull and indistinct.

Or again, look at Fig. 21 or Fig. 22 for 25 seconds and then go back at once to Fig. 20. You will find that the cross now seen first is most likely to be the one at which you have just been looking, and that for a short time it tends to change less easily and rapidly into the other one. But this effect soon wears off.

Instead of drawing the figure on a flat surface, make a model in plasticine, or wood, or any other suitable material, so that one cross appears in actual relief upon the other. The whole appearance now becomes very much more stable indeed. And if a stereoscopic slide is made, so that either cross appears at a different distance from the other, the figure will remain stable for as long as the binocular combination can be held.

It seems as if we may conclude that the stability of a reversible figure may depend partly on the area of fixation, and is greatest when the observer is looking steadily at an area of minimum overlap of neighbouring shapes. Further, stability may be increased by anything that makes one of the figures appear bright or striking relatively to the other. And again, if the observer first attends for a short time to one only of the alternative shapes of a reversible figure, this is the one that will tend to appear first and, within limits, to persist longest if, immediately afterwards, he looks at the complete figure. But all of these only diminish or postpone the instability; they do not get rid of it.

The most important thing seems to be the provision of fixed points of reference on some kind of a distance scale which gives to things seen the appearance of solidity. When that is arranged figures of the reversible cross type become very much more stable indeed.

A most interesting illustration of this last point is to be found in the little wooden models of their favourite leaders which people sometimes carried about with them during a stage of the French Revolution, when it was not always safe to let everybody know one's political party. Compare the photograph of the model with that of the silhouette in the picture shown in Fig. 23 (opposite p. 80). Or better still, turn up a model for yourself on a lathe and then cast a shadow of it on a light background. It is very difficult indeed to see the human profile in the model, with its solid appearance, and almost equally difficult to avoid seeing it in the flat shadow.

Fig. 23.

Now look at the next series of figures (Fig. 24), attending to each form for about a minute. *A* reverses beautifully and is seen alternately as a cylinder standing on its base or lying on one side. *B* is immediately seen as a jug, but this does practically nothing to stop its reversibility, though just what happens to the "handle" and the "spout" when they are seen at the bottom of the figure is not easy to say. *C* is still more decidedly a jug, but yet the central cylinder goes on reversing as before, though either the curved sides of the jug become redundant when the cylinder is seen lying down, or the jug is treated as if it were standing behind the cylinder, and a separate object. *D* is curious, for either it is seen as a rather odd sort of vessel standing upright and with a circle inscribed on its side, or the whole thing tilts over and becomes a single figure of which the circle forms the bottom. But when we saw all these representations in the lectures nearly everybody agreed that reversibility stopped completely with *E* so far as the figure as a whole is concerned, though a very little possible change of position remained. For now only a part of one of the original two circles remains, and this can be treated as a portion of the base of the jug, the remainder being obscured, or as a rather odd and unusual feature on the top. Anybody who likes can pursue this series a little further and he will find that he gets the figure more and more firmly stabilized, as he introduces more and more partially obscured features, that is to say as he gets into the drawing more and more appearance of solidity.

We can now leave these representations in the flat and go again into the outside world, the street, the playing-field, the school, and the factory. Here objects as they normally appear have all those qualities that we have seen may lend two-dimensional representations stability. Our fixation points vary freely and rapidly; nearly all the things we see have some special marked features; observa-

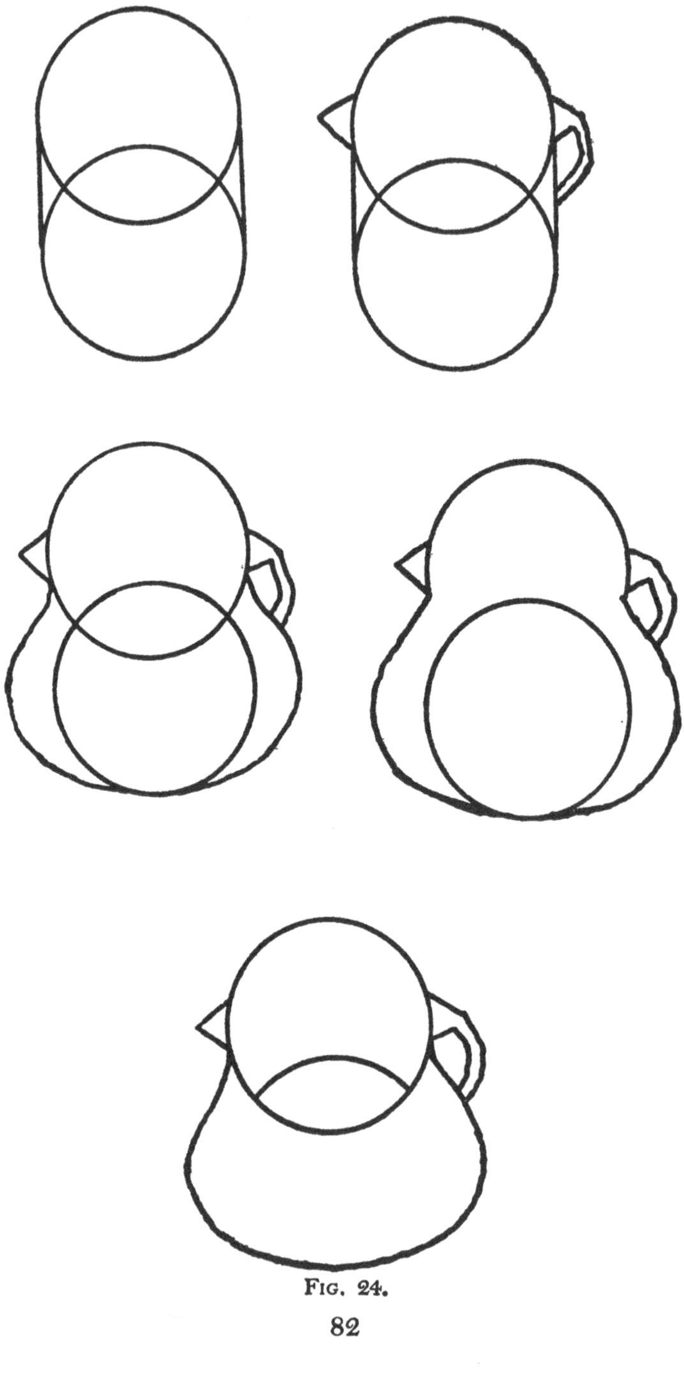

FIG. 24.

tion is not usually of something singled out from everything else, but proceeds in a sequence so that we turn to one thing from another with something already in our mind; above all we are in a world in which we can use fixed points of reference on a distance-scale. There are, of course many other influences at work of which probably the most important are the names that can be used as a check upon observation by one person for another; but these are the most important visual conditions which work against ambiguity and reversibility in everyday life.

2. REVERSIBLE MOVEMENT

Perhaps the most interesting and puzzling of all the instances of reversible appearances of a single object is the case of the rotating vane. Anybody can very easily fit this up and do some experiments, and he may be able to find out some things that so far are not known for certain. Fit a small vane on the head of a shaft which can be rotated, preferably at a wide variety of speed, by any kind of motor. To get the best effect throw a shadow of the vane and shaft on a ground glass screen. Set the vane rotating and go a little distance away and watch it. The shadow is perhaps seen to be going round in a clockwise direction, but as you watch it all of a sudden it reverses to an anti-clockwise movement, and then a moment later may be it seems to stop going round and to jump rapidly in and out like a concertina. There are a lot of other things that the rotating vane can seem to do, and it is worthwhile watching it for some time and making a list of all that you see.

With a little ingenuity you can produce a silent switch which will actually reverse the direction of movement of the vane, and then you can get somebody else to help and he can use the switch at irregular intervals and without giving any notice. It makes no difference. An actual change of direction of rotation may pass unnoticed altogether, or an apparent change may be noticed just at the same time but in a precisely opposite sense. The concertina effect, and all the other possible interpretations are left completely unaffected.

Nobody seems to have succeeded so far in finding out how to control this extremely unstable observation. An observer may use one eye or two. Any variety of fixed points of reference can be drawn on the screen. Sections or strips of the moving shadow can be obscured. Foregrounds or backgrounds giving fixed points of distance from the observer can be introduced. Speeds of movement can be widely varied. All these and many other dodges have been tried but still no important difference in the liability to reversion has been demonstrated.

Yet still it seems as if there must be some simple device which will do what is wanted, and if only we could find out we should know more than we do about the conditions that make it possible to observe and judge consistently and accurately directions and changes of movement which involve depth or distance. Moreover, it does seem as if the conditions ought to be something like those which have most to do with the control of reversibility in the case of the motionless figure, and to lie in the provision of a foreground and background which contain fixed depth points that can be used as standards for reference at critical stages of the apparent movement.

Meanwhile it is certainly the case that even in everyday life movements towards or away from us are very difficult to judge accurately when they exceed a certain amount or go on in the same direction for more than a short time. And at night, when surrounding objects are dimmed or blacked out they are the most difficult of all. We are, indeed, forced to conclude that the visual perception of movement, especially in the third dimension, is one of the many apparently simple things in human observation that we still know little about. When more than one object is moving in a fairly limited area at the same time, everybody must have noticed the difficulties of interpretation that occur.

3. CHANGE OF MOVEMENT

A very peculiar thing about reversible figures is that when one shape or interpretation changes into another and back again, nobody can see either in process of changing. One is there, and then, after a bit, another is there; but there is no movement from one to the other. And so, of course, nobody ever supposes that one of the shapes or interpretations accounts for, or itself produces, the other, although it can quite regularly be followed by the other in experience.

In fact it seems as if our observation naturally treats one thing as the cause of another only when there is not only change in both but also actual movement, in the sense that both are seen to change their positions. And also the positions which are observed in the thing that is treated as an effect must be different from those of whatever is treated as the cause. All science is an attempt to discover causes, and so let us look a little more closely at the ways in which we can observe things moving from one spot to another.

It is easy enough to see movement when in fact no real movement occurs. Make a closed box and put a lamp in it. Then make a pin-hole in one side of the box and set it up in an otherwise completely dark room. Stand a few feet away and look at the pin point of light, preferably "out of the corner of your eye," as we say. In a moment or two the small light will seem to move, making sudden little darts sometimes in one direction and sometimes in another. This appearance of movement is called the "autokinetic illusion," and although many people have tried, nobody has completely explained it. It has been known for many hundreds of years and was, in fact, recorded by star-gazers in the ancient Arabian deserts.

You can see it, indeed, on any clear, starlit night, if you like to look sideways at some not very bright star in a clear patch of sky. An odd thing about this observation is that, although the small light is most certainly seen to move, yet it does not appear as genuinely changing its position.

This apparent movement, however, can be as easily controlled as it can be produced. Two neighbouring pin-points will appear to move less than one, and three less than two, and if we go on adding points in a pattern we soon come to the stage in which there is no apparent movement at all. The whole thing is, in fact, one more illustration of how in order that the senses and judgment can give decisive and definite information we must have fixed points of reference, which then have a strong "anchoring" effect upon whatever is seen.

Now try another experiment. Take two pin-point boxes with a switch for each light. Place the boxes at the same height and about a foot from one another. Then switch on the lights alternatively, and if you vary the intervals a bit you will soon hit on one which gives a very strong impression of a light in one position moving to the other one, and so back and forth as you continue the experiment. If you observe very carefully you will probably see that the light does not seem to move quite to the extreme positions of either pin-point, but reverses when it is still a little short of these. Also sometimes the path of the movement may appear slightly curved, dropping or rising a little towards its mid-point. The little light may even seem to disappear in the middle, as if it goes into a tunnel, and then to reappear on the other side. There are a great many interesting things that can be observed in this experiment, as you vary the distance of the two lights, their brightness, and the interval of successive exposure. It is not in the least necessary to have lights or pin-points, of course. Any display in almost any colour or shape can be used, provided the appropriate intervals of successive exposure are arranged. A vertical line, for example, may seem to fall into a horizontal position and then rise again. The whole thing is, of course, simply an elementary illustration of the familiar principle of cinematograph display.

Is it possible to distinguish directly between this kind of appearance of movement and what we call "real" movement under comparable conditions? There is still disagreement about this, and you should try the experiment for yourself and try to make up your own mind. Of course, somebody else will have to act as the observer, for the latter must not know anything except what he can gather from the appearance of movement itself about the conditions of the experiment. Probably there is some difference, and this is connected, as with many of the other things that we have been considering in this chapter, with a certain lack of stability in the case of the apparent movement. A very little change of conditions may make the whole thing look different and make the observer a little doubtful and puzzled. But although this is the case with lights, or with simple lines and geometrical figures, all such doubtfulness disappears if the objects that are successively exposed within the limits of the correct intervals are representations of things which we have seen over and over again to move in the ways that are indicated.

In both of the two cases that we have just been considering, what is treated as a single thing seems to move from one position to another, and then either to reappear in the original place, or to move back to it again. But the most interesting case of all is when a movement of one thing is seen as introductory to a movement of another. This can, of course, be represented in a moving picture, but it is safe enough to say that we all meet with it first in real life and with the real movements of solid objects. It also seems safe enough to say that the very first time anybody sees this happen he treats the first moving object as in some way specially connected with the movement of the second.

4. MOVEMENT AND CAUSATION

Take about two feet of flat wooden board and cut a narrow and shallow groove running from one end to the other. About half-way along make a small cup depression just deep enough to hold a marble or a steel ball-bearing, but not deep enough to keep it from moving if it is hit by another one. Prop the board at one end to make a slightly inclined plane. Put one marble, or ball-bearing, in the little cup and start a second one rolling down the groove from the top of the incline. The two balls will, of course, bump together, and then the one in the cup will begin to move and both will roll down the incline.

It may seem to us that there is nothing remarkable in all this. We have seen this sort of thing over and over again, and what happens is just what we expect to happen. But, as a matter of fact, when the two balls come together and the one that was stationary is seen to move, the whole relation of the other one to it is also seen to change, and the ball that started from the top is observed as actively "launching" the hitherto motionless ball. The two movements in sequence are connected together by the mind in a very special way.

There is a lot to be said for the view that seeing movements of solid objects follow one another after impact, gives us the simplest possible instance of causation which is directly observed, and that this observation is a natural one, made at once by the senses and the mind as soon as the appropriate conditions are witnessed. But before we go on let us try a few more experiments.

Get a couple of electric railway coaches and weight them a little so as to make them fairly stable. Have about twelve feet of line. Now build up the circuit as indicated in Fig. 25. It will be best to arrange a remote control and

CIRCUIT DIAGRAM OF APPARATUS FOR STUDYING THE PERCEPTION OF CAUSAL RELATIONSHIPS BETWEEN TWO MOVING OBJECTS

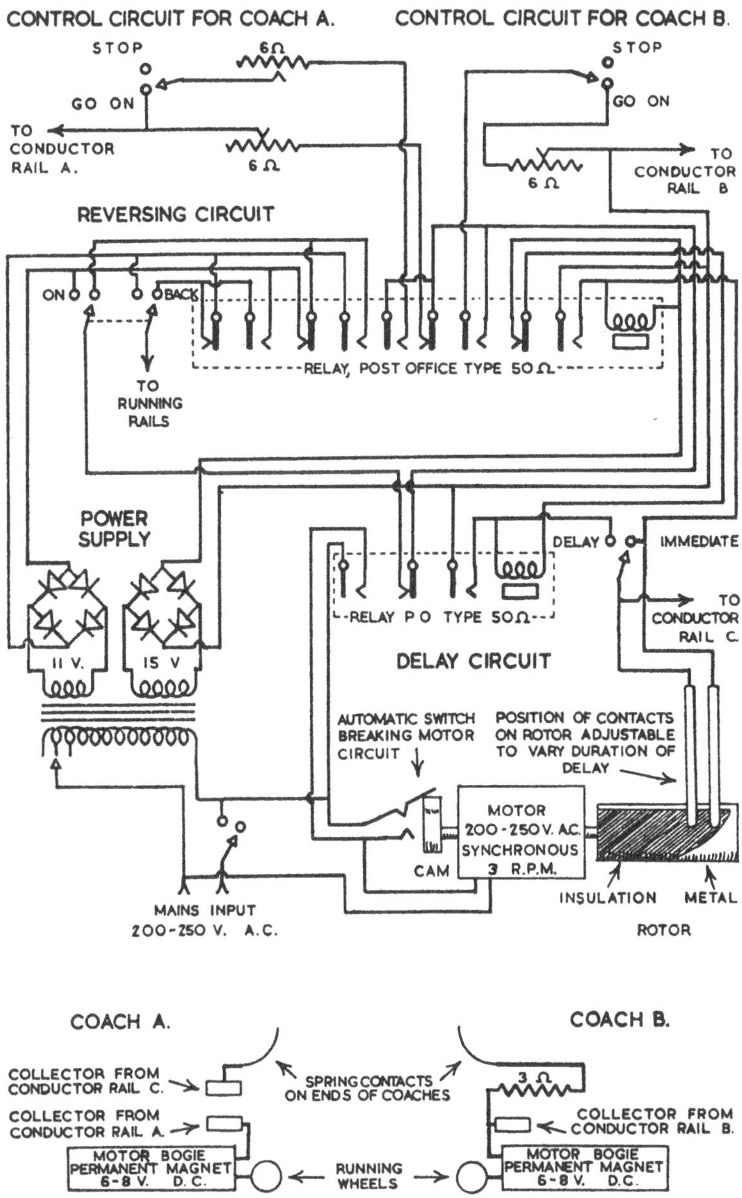

Fig. 25.

to have the actual control mechanism out of sight, for this will make the observations that are required easier to make and much more striking. One of the coaches stands half-way along the line and the other is placed at one end. With this arrangement you can make the two coaches do all sorts of things. Practise a little until you are sure that you can move them exactly as you wish. Then assemble your audience. Say that one of the coaches will be made to move and then something will happen to the other or perhaps to both of them. The observers are to try to notice all those cases, if there are any, in which the first moving coach is seen to be connected with, for example to produce, or account for, the subsequent events.

Try all of the following sequences in any order you like. We call the coach that starts from the end of the line coach "A" and the other coach "B."

1. Coach A moves with moderate speed, collides with coach B and both move off to the stop at the far end of the rails.

2. Coach A moves out as slowly as possible, collides with coach B which then moves at maximum speed to the stop at the far end.

3. Coach A moves out at maximum speed, collides with coach B; which then moves as slowly as possible to the stop at the far end.

4. Coach A moves out at normal speed, collides with coach B; nothing further happens for two seconds and then both coaches move smartly away to the stop at the far end.

5. Coach A moves out slowly, collides gently with B and immediately reverses at top speed to the stop at the starting end of the line.

6. Coach A moves out at moderate speed, collides with B; nothing happens for two seconds and then both move away slowly together back to the starting point.

There are, as will be seen, many other combinations that can be tried, and all of them are interesting and instructive.

Of course, any audience that can be got together nowadays is almost sure to know a lot about the possibilities of electrical control, but if they will play the game properly, as they usually will, and really try to look at the sequences you produce as nearly as possible wholly from the point of view of what they can see, Case 1 will stand away from all of the others as if what is seen itself satisfies everything, and there is no need to ask any more questions. Coach A can be and usually will be treated, without any more ado, as if it sets coach B moving, and it does not seem as if there is any difference in the readiness and certainty of this observation, whether those who make it have or have not seen actual railway coaches doing this sort of thing over and over again in shunting operations.

But all the other cases, from 2 to 6 include something which from the point of view of immediate observation seems to be odd and questionable. Something seems to be coming into play which cannot be put down simply to the prior movement of A and the impact with B. Clearly we do not connect two series of happenings as cause and effect merely because they follow one another, or even simply because they follow one another in very much the same way a large number of times. The interval between the succession, and the speed and direction of the secondary changes in relation to the primary ones, are equally important. So may be the range and number of objects or items of observation that are affected.

What would have happened to an experiment like the one we have just done if in fact every time we had ever seen one object move and come into contact with another, after an interval of about two seconds, both objects had been observed to move slowly back along the path of the first one? There seems no reason to doubt that, if that had happened to us, Case 6, in the alternatives we tried, would have been the one we should all have picked out at once as satisfactory, and requiring no further question. We should have treated the movement of A and its collision with B as the observed cause of the reverse movement after an interval, of both A and B. But this would mean only that the particular conditions under which what is at once treated as cause is identified by observation as depending on the repetition of special sequences of change a large number of times. It seems, in fact, that that kind of connection of one thing with another which we call causation is directly observed, and also as if the direct observation is closely tied up with movement sequences; but that the particular range of conditions under which one thing will, in fact, be observed by practically everybody as the cause of another is decided by constant repetition in experience. To put this in another way, given the appropriate circumstances, the observing mind immediately connects one thing with another and treats one as in some special manner the explanation of the other. But at the same time it is true to say that the particular circumstances, or class of circumstances, in which this happens does depend, as many people have pointed out, upon frequent repetition in experience.

It goes without saying perhaps that the *idea* of causation, and all the other kinds of ideas of connection between things and events which science, as we know it, uses, have developed slowly and as a result of careful analysis and experiment, following on that kind of immediate observation which we made with the inclined plane or the railway coaches. In this way the mind of the trained scientist connects things together whose relation could certainly not be observed by the unaided operations of the senses. And also a good many things that immediate sensory observation connects by way of cause and effect, later on are not treated in this direct and simple manner, but are considered to be mistakes.

Yet elaborate connections between one event and another which make up the orderly world of science start from the simple fact that all everyday observation is of sequences and series of things, and that the mind not only records qualities, and places, and times, but also connects one thing with another. Later we shall be trying to discover exactly what happens when the mind thinks, and then we shall find that thinking is closely bound up with this basic process of attributing connections, and is in fact chiefly concerned with filling up gaps which direct observation seems to leave empty.

We have, as everybody knows, other ways of connecting one thing with another besides treating them as causally related. We can see one thing as an instance of a class, or as merely following or preceding another, as a stage in a regular process of growth, as related within some system of kinship, or even as an odd and accidental occurrence. In all of these, and with many other kinds of connection, it is interesting and instructive to look for the most characteristic condition of direct observation in which the type of relation concerned seems to be made naturally. The principle is always the same. Just as causation seems to be specially connected with the observation of real movements in sequence after contact, so there are typical conditions under which the observing mind makes the other connections that are later elaborated and refined.

5. CONCLUSIONS

1. If we take reversible figures which do not involve moving parts and try to stabilize them, we find the important points to be (*a*) the area of fixation, (*b*) the degree of striking contrast between one part and another, (*c*) whether we have just been attending to one interpretation of the alternatives presented alone, and especially, (*d*) whether we can provide fixed points on a distance-scale against which the parts of the figure concerned can be estimated, that is whether we can produce in the figure concerned the appearance of solidity.

2. If the reversible figure contains moving parts it seems much more difficult to stabilize it, but probably the necessary operation is the same one, of giving it a solid appearance.

3. Movement can appear to occur when in fact it can easily be demonstrated that what is alleged to move has been stationary all the time. Two special cases of this are the autokinetic illusion and the "phi-phenomenon."[1] The first can very easily be controlled, and the second requires a rather limited and special range of conditions.

4. When solid objects are seen to move, and when the movement of one brings it into observable contact with another, which then also begins to move, the first movement is often immediately treated as in some special way connected with the second and the cause of it.

5. But it is not simply the sequence of actual movements which occasions this observation; the interval between the successive movements and the relative speeds and directions of the movement series also play important parts.

6. It seems highly probable that the idea of cause and effect, which is the most important of all the ideas used in natural science, is based upon this simple and direct ability of the mind to connect together things that are observed as a sequence of solid objects in movement. But at the same time what particular sequences are regarded as causally related depends upon frequent repetition in experience. And in any case the idea of cause as it is used in scientific explanation demands considerable analysis and refinement of the basic observation.

7. All normal observation in everyday life is of series and sequences of things and events, and the mind not only observes the descriptive qualities of the things and events, but also connects them together in a variety of ways.

[1] This is the technical name given to the second case of apparent movement described in Section 3 of this chapter.

CHAPTER FIVE

The Mind Remembers

Everything that we do involves remembering in one form or another. If we try to make an absolute measurement, our only way is to use some kind of standard which has been built up on a basis of experience. If we use scales and fixed points for measurement, we directly observe only a bit of them, and fill up what is needed of the rest from memory. If we have to make a series of movements, our senses respond to the signal that starts them and some, or all, of the rest comes from the results of past actions. When the mind observes, always some of our report is based upon what we ourselves bring with us to the task. If we connect one event with another one, at the most only a part of what we are dealing with is externally present at the time. We must therefore now ask how far it is possible to do experiments on remembering and to find out something definite about the conditions which make it succeed or fail. Perhaps the answer to this question may help us to learn something about how best to arrange and to study things that we really want to be able to recall.

1. REMEMBERING IN WHAT SEEMS TO BE DIRECT OBSERVATION

Here is an easy and interesting experiment. Get a few blank cards and on each of them write clearly a single phrase like:

All is not gild that glotters;
Talcer Powdum;
The Royal Intuition;
Fish and Chops.

Collect whatever audience you can, expose the phrases for a brief single glance, and get observers to write down what they have seen. We did this in the Royal Institution lectures. Out of 140 cards returned, 3 correctly reported *All is not gild that glotters*, 54 reported *All is not gold that glitters*, and the remaining ones reported other inaccurate variations; 33 reported *Talcer Powdum*, and 65 of the others gave *Talcum Powder* as the original; 5 returned *The Royal Intuition*, and 103 *The Royal Institution*; 28 gave *Fish and Chops*, 97 *Fish and Chips*. Familiar and remembered forms are obviously overpowering the immediate work of the eyes. Some of the alternatives sent in for *The Royal Intuition* were especially interesting. Among them were *The Royal Wedding*, *The Royal Baby*, *The Royal Christening*. Moreover, that 103 out of 140 people were prepared to say that they had seen *The Royal Institution* when they had not, shows the enormous influence upon immediate recall that the setting of an observation can have.

It is, of course, by no means necessary that remembering should falsify observation, for it is just as easy to show that familiar words, phrases, or passages can be reported correctly with much shorter exposures than are needed in other cases. Only a bit of what is there has to be read, and the rest is remembered.

2. THE CURVE OF FORGETTING

The first really well-controlled experiments on remembering were done by Ebbinghaus, a German psychologist, and published in 1885. If we make a list of ordinary words and set people to try to learn and remember them, some people may know some of the words very well to begin with, others may know a different selection, and others may know none at all. It would be like setting competitors to run a race without paying any attention to handicapping. Ebbinghaus wondered whether there was some way in which he could reduce all people to exactly the same level to begin with. He hit upon the bright idea of using nonsense syllables. You write down two consonants with a gap and then put a vowel between so as to make a meaningless three-letter word. In this way you can make a list of meaningless three-letter words of any desired length. You have to make sure that no word starts with the same or the next alphabetical letter as the one just before it. You must avoid having successive words that rhyme, and there are various other precautions that must be taken, most of which anybody can work out for himself. Only one word must be seen at a time by the learner and each word for the same length of time.

Ebbinghaus set himself to learn lists of this kind, repeating each syllable at sight until he came to the end of the list, and then trying to repeat the whole list from memory. He reckoned a list learned when he managed to produce the first completely accurate repetition of a whole list. He then allowed various intervals to elapse and found out how much time was saved in relearning. From this he worked out his famous "curve of forgetting" (see Fig. 26). We can see that there is a very rapid fall in the amount that is remembered immediately after the first learning, but that the rate of forgetting then slows up, and after two days there is very little further loss.

Of course, it rarely happens that any material that we try to learn by heart is as lacking in meaning as that which Ebbinghaus used. If lists of ordinary words are learned the rate at which they are forgotten is considerably slower, and the period of greatest loss comes later. But with all types of verbal material there is apt to be a marked fall off of remembering very soon after it is just learned. Cramming the memory is, in fact, hardly ever, except by good luck or accident, a profitable thing to do.

It seems odd at first that we are very likely to forget items that we have made a special effort to remember.

We hardly ever make such an effort, in fact, unless for some reason we find the items difficult to deal with, and are afraid that we are going to forget them. It seems as if this first impression of "I shall never be able to remember that" is more effective than any following decision to try especially hard.

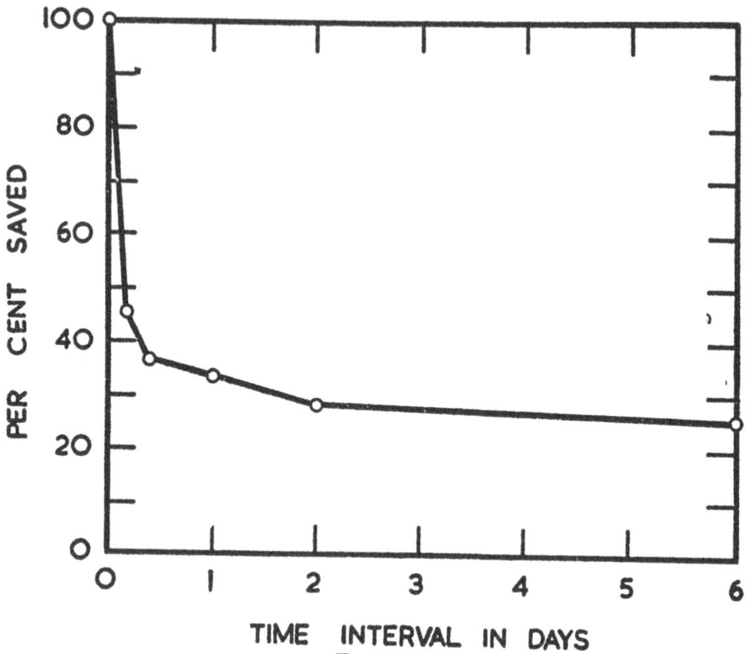

FIG. 26.

When the mind is building up material to be remembered, it often seems to work like people who are building a bridge across a river and who begin on the two banks and proceed towards the middle. If all the items have about equal weight, those near the beginning and those near the end are likely to be the first to be established, and those towards the middle the last. So if lists are being learned and there are items which appear to be particularly difficult, it is generally best to deal with them, not by trying to make an extra special effort, but to put them, if this can be done, in the privileged positions, and then treat them like all the others.

This peculiarity of early and late items seems to be connected in some way with the thing that we found some time ago, that on the whole the first and last parts of words are better seen, and more accurately reported, than the middle parts. It certainly is related to another difficulty that bothers a lot of folks, especially when they are getting oldish, that if they have to try to recall a proper name, they can often remember the initial letter, but nothing else.

It is sometimes said that a restful sleep stops forgetting. So we may be advised to learn anything we want to remember a bit before normal sleeping time, and then we shall wake up and find that it all remains bright and clear. There is certainly something in this. It has often been tried experimentally and the general result has been to show that sleep does arrest the ordinary process of forgetting. It may well be, but this is a little less certain, that the longer anything is retained after learning, the longer after this it is likely to remain available for recall. If this is the case, sleep, by arresting forgetting, actually prolongs remembering. But it will not do to count for certain on this happening.

3. SOME FURTHER POINTS ABOUT EXACT RECALL

Judging by the amount of work that has been done on the subject, it would seem that most folks who have been interested in the study of memory have thought that exact and literal recall is the really important thing. We shall soon have to begin to consider whether this is in fact the case; but before we do that, there are a few from among the many other facts that have been established by experiments on learning by heart to which we ought to pay attention.

Not seldom we are set to work to learn something, knowing that we are likely to have to make use of it on, or up to, a certain date, but that after this it will not matter very much. Then we may find that when the date has passed, the ease and efficiency with which we forget what we have learned are quite remarkable. How much this is due to the fact that under these circumstances we are very likely to think about and go over the material at odd moments up to the required date, and then to drop such revision completely, nobody knows. It is, however, quite certain that the length of a memory can be considerably affected, within fairly wide limits of time, by the frame of mind with which we approach its learning.

There may well be some connection between this and another problem that has been widely studied and is usually known as the "distribution of practice." Most people find that if they have rather long lists, or difficult verbal material, to learn they can establish it quicker and retain it longer if they distribute their learning over a number of short periods instead of massing it all in one spell of the same total duration. In technical language, for this kind of verbal material, "distributed" practice is more economical than "massed practice."

It is possible that this is not so simple and direct a result as it is frequently taken to be. Perhaps a partial learning, which distributed practice always means, makes people more inclined to call up the whole topic to mind at odd moments, and to start a kind of unplanned revision from time to time, whereas learning all at one go, which is what massed practice is to be taken to mean, does not do this.

It has been shown many times that if a job is begun, but interrupted, most folks start it up again, naturally and without any definite decision, as soon as they can. But if a job is completed, or seems to be completed, before it is stopped, this does not happen to anything like the same extent. Whatever may be the explanation, in verbal learning, when exact repetition is required, a distributed and intermittent practice seems to be the best.

4. REMEMBERING IN EVERYDAY LIFE

As a matter of fact, for ordinary purposes, very exact repetition is more of a hindrance than a help. Generally we have to use what we can remember to help us to do something different that has cropped up. Except in school life, and for the purpose of most formal examinations, if we want literally exact repetition we can look up fixed records of some sort. Before exact and permanent records were kept, if society demanded exact repetition, as it did on many ceremonial occasions, it had to make use of special devices like rhyming phrases, or song, or dance cycles which, for some reason, naturally preserved a standard form and order relatively easily. And if an individual wants to remember any series of items or events literally and in order, he often finds it useful to invent some special device, such as putting them into a verse form in the correct sequence, or even making a tune about them; or he may link up items or events which he finds difficult to recall with others that he finds easy. For we have to recognize that, though people talk about a "good memory," in actual fact the ability to recall accurately is almost always specialized. Some people can remember words best, or words having to do with special topics; or pictures; or numbers; and may be good at the one and very bad at the others. If circumstances demand that they should remember material which is given to them in a form which is, for them, a bad one, they can often improve the chance of accurate memory by finding equivalent forms that are, for them, good ones, and associating the two. But these aids to memory are not, as a rule, very helpful unless a person invents them for himself, and also they lose their effectiveness if they are frequently or extensively used.

In any case these special tricks cannot be much exploited in ordinary life. As a general rule when things happen to us one after another, we do not even know which of them are likely to be of the greatest use to us in the future. They all go into some general, bunched-up mass of more or less available experience, and when we say that we remember them what we really mean is that, if the need arises, we can reconstruct the right things from this mass of experience, not necessarily in the exact form in which they occurred, but in a form that will help us to find a suitable answer to some problem that is important at the moment.

So we must try to find out what happens to remembering when we see or hear a thing once, and then, without any definite effort to learn it by heart, try to repeat its substance but not necessarily its exact sequence, or its literally unchanged description. Some most surprising things do happen, particularly if the record passes from person to person in a series.

5. AN EXPERIMENT IN SERIAL REMEMBERING

In the course of everyday life we may see something happen and then a little later describe it to somebody else, who soon passes on the story to a third person, and so the report goes on, until perhaps it reaches a form which lots of people repeat without much further change. This is a way in which rumours spread, in which opinions may be formed, but in which all the time people's memories claim, and appear, to be at work. There is, as everybody will know, a popular kind of game which turns this process into an experiment. This is how we tried the experiment in the lectures.

We got a number of volunteers from the audience and sent them all out of the room but one. We then put up a large picture, and brought the second person into the room. All the audience and the first person could see the picture, but the second person could not. The first person, looking at the picture all the time, tried to describe it clearly to the second, and a record was made of the description. The third person now came in and the second, still without any sight of the picture, passed on his version of the description. When he had completed this, the second person joined the audience, and could look at the picture; but, of course, at this stage he was not allowed to alter in any way the description which he had completed. In this way successive descriptions passed from one to another through the group of observers. Each attempt was sound-recorded, and here is our first series exactly reproduced. Description number 1 was made while the speaker was looking at the picture, but number 2 and all the rest were made without any direct visual observation.

1. There is a cat, and fairly near the middle, more to the right, there is a bird-cage with a bird in it, just above it, but a little to the left; and on the left is a vase of flowers with some leaves in it, too; and in front of that is a red book with some cards on it, plain cards; and to the right is a bottle of ink. All these things, the vase, the cat, and the bottle of ink are on a table with a blue cloth, and above the cage, in the middle, there is a sort of notice saying, "A Bird Fancier," in inverted commas, hanging up.

2. In the picture there is a table. In the centre of the table, but a little to the right, is a cat. Just above the cat, a little to the right still, is a bird-cage, and to the left of the picture is a vase of flowers, and in front of that is a red book. To the right of that is a bottle of ink. Above the bird cage is a notice which says, "The Bird Fancier," in inverted commas.

3. In the middle of the picture there is a table. To the left of the table is a bird-cage and above the bird-cage there is a notice saying, "Bird Fancier," in inverted commas. Still to the left there is a red book and a bottle of ink.

4. In the centre of the picture there is a table. To the right of the table is a bird-cage, and over the bird-cage is something written in—surrounded by—inverted commas. There is a bottle of ink on the table.

5. In the centre of the picture is a table. On the right of the picture there is a bird-cage. On the top of the bird-cage there is some words in inverted commas.

6. In the centre of the picture is a table. On top of the table is a bird-cage, above which are words in inverted commas.

When we study this short sequence of reports, the first thing that is likely to strike us is what a lot everybody seems to have forgotten. More interesting are the kinds of things that are lost and how they drop out. Relative positions seem to be very unstable. The bird-cage moves from right middle, to right, then to left, then to right again, stays there for two attempts, and then loses specific position entirely and is described as "on top of the table," a phrase which most people would certainly take to mean "in the middle." All colours but one are forgotten immediately and that one speedily follows suit. The title is lost. All incidental details disappear, and even the cat, twice mentioned in the initial attempt, has no place after the second narrator has done his bit. From the final attempt it would still be possible to reconstruct a picture which would have some kind of general descriptive likeness to the original, but that is all.

Let us now consider a second series obtained in just the same way, but a little longer, and produced by somewhat older observers.

1. The scene is of the inside of what might be a stable or wooden house of some sort. At the top of the picture is a roof, probably made of boards. In the background there is a framework structure of boards, then a complete background of boards at the back of the house. To the right-hand side the wood at the end of the house comes towards you. There is a doorway through which you can see a waterwheel. Outside the doorway runs a stream. In the foreground of the picture there are a lot of wooden and metal structures. In the picture there are two people, on the left a woman pushing a wheelbarrow containing some stones. On the right is a man, possibly a blacksmith, holding in his hand some tongs in which is a piece of metal, on an anvil. In the distance to the left of the picture a woman is disappearing through a doorway, and above her head, to the right, perched on a bar, is some sort of a bird.

2. The picture seems to be of a stable, a wooden stable, which has a wooden roof. There is a wooden frame half-way through the picture behind which is a frame of boards. The

right wall comes towards the observer, and it shows a door through which one can see a waterwheel and stream. There are two people inside the house, a woman with a wheelbarrow in which there are stones, and a blacksmith holding a piece of metal on an anvil with tongs. In the foreground are some wooden and metal structures. In the left-hand corner of the picture there is a woman disappearing through a door, and on top of the door is a strut on which a bird is perched.

3. There is a wooden stable with a wooden framework behind it. The right wall comes to the observer, and through a door one can see a waterwheel turning some water. Two people are in the middle of the picture, one is a woman with a wheelbarrow full of stones, and the other is a blacksmith holding a piece of metal by tongs on an anvil. To the left-hand side of the picture there is a woman disappearing out of a door. Above the door is a strut on which is a bird.

4. In the centre of the picture there is a stable. There is a wooden partition in the middle of the stable, and behind it a wooden frame. On the right, in the wall, there is a door and through the door there is a waterwheel with some water. In the foreground there are two people. One is a woman with a wheelbarrow full of stones, but there is also a man, a blacksmith holding a piece of metal with tongs, striking on an anvil. On the left-hand side there is a door and through the door a woman is disappearing. Over the door is a strut on which is sitting a bird.

5. In the centre of the picture is a stable, and in the centre of that there is a wooden partition with a wooden frame behind it. On the right-hand wall there is a door. On the left-hand side of the picture there is another door with a woman disappearing into it. In the front of the picture there are two people, a man and a woman. The woman is holding a wheelbarrow full of stones. The man, who appears to be a blacksmith, is holding an anvil and knocking a stone with it.

6. In the centre of the picture is a stable. In the centre of the stable there is a wooden frame. In the right-hand side of the stable there is a door, and on the left-hand side another door with a woman disappearing into it. In the foreground there is a man and a woman. The woman has a wheelbarrow full of stones and the man appears to be a blacksmith and is holding an anvil and hitting a stone with it.

7. In the centre of the picture there is a stable. In the centre

of the stable there is a wooden frame. To the right of the stable there is a door and to the left there is another door through which a woman is disappearing. In the front of the picture there are two people, a woman who is wheeling a wheelbarrow full of stones and a man who looks like a blacksmith and is hitting an anvil with a stone.

8. In the centre of the picture there is a stable with a wooden frame. On either side of the stable there is a door. Through the left-hand door a woman is just disappearing. In the front of this view there is a woman with a barrowload of stones and a man who looks like a blacksmith, hitting an anvil with a stone.

9. In the picture there is a stable, with wooden framework. There are two doors to the stable and into one of them a woman is just disappearing. There is a blacksmith in the picture and he is striking an anvil with a piece of stone.

10. In the picture there is a stable with a wooden frame. A woman is just disappearing through the door. The blacksmith is inside, hitting an anvil with a piece of stone.

There is exactly the same remarkable process of immediate forgetting, and, in general, it follows a similar pattern. Positions are simplified, changed, and drop out. There is the same progressive omission of incidental detail, with a few items remaining dominant, in the first series the table, the bird-cage and words; in the second series the stable, two people, and an anvil.

One or two details in this series are particularly interesting because they suggest why some kinds of report are especially likely to change or disappear. The first description of all says that there are two people in the picture and then goes on to refer to three. The very first attempted recall regularizes this by putting two people inside the house and a third going out. But still perhaps it seems a bit odd to have a woman with a wheelbarrow full of stones inside a "house" which has also been described as a "stable." The "house" is left out and the two people come into "the middle of the picture." Observer number 4 now makes the blacksmith strike "on an anvil," which is, of course, a natural thing for him to do. But the next attempt lays a foundation for some more important changes by dropping the blacksmith's tongs, replacing them by a stone (presumably from the wheelbarrow) and making the man hold an anvil and knock a stone with it. This seems a surprising thing to do, and before long the relation is reversed and the blacksmith is "hitting an anvil with a stone." Finally the woman with the wheelbarrow disappears, a single stone remains, and the blacksmith is merely using the stone as a hammer.

Once again it would be possible to reconstruct a picture from the final description which would have a general resemblance to the original, but that is all.

If you like to plan a whole series of experiments of this kind you will find the same characteristics coming out over and over again: a tendency to leave out disconnected details, or to link them up so that they appear simply as a sort of list or inventory of objects; a great amount of inaccuracy concerning relative positions, with a strong tendency to put one or two things somewhere in the middle and eventually to omit the rest; a great amount of confusion and forgetting of the qualities of objects, especially of colours, sizes, and shapes; a strong likelihood that titles and names will be forgotten and phrases altered; an equally strong probability that unusual and odd relationships—such as holding an anvil and hitting a stone with it—will be preserved for a while, but will eventually either disappear completely, or be changed into something more in line with normal experience. It is interesting to try a few instances in which number is seen to play an important part. For then it often happens that the numbers will be exaggerated, especially if, in the original, they go a little beyond what (p. 59) we found to be within the normal span. Usually in the end we reach a version which has some sort of a general family likeness to the original, but sometimes even this is lost and we get a form that nobody in the world would be able, without special information, to match with the first one.

There are a great many variations of this game which can be introduced, though only a few of them have been tried experimentally. For example, when we come to the end of the series we can get all the observers to discuss and argue together about what they have been reporting, and to produce an agreed reconstruction of the original—what they agree that it must have been, not necessarily what they remember to have heard that it was. Or somewhere in the series we can embark on a cross-examination, suggesting things that were left out, or that were never reported, or even present, at all; or questioning things that have been kept in. At some point we can introduce a new picture or a new description, identical with the first in some respects and different in others, and see what then happens. We can let a number of people see or hear the original, describe it, and then argue and try to convince one another about their differences. Obviously there are many other variations that could be tried, and from all of them we can learn something about the character and course of everyday remembering.

In one respect, however informal we make this game, or experiment, its results are likely to differ from those of the free and easy use of remembering of daily life, whether the recall is individual, or a sequence in which many persons play their parts. Omissions are likely to be more prominent and inventions less. But even in our small series, we had one or two inventions, and if we had begun with material that was dramatic, or comical, or if, as has been said already, numbers above five or six had been important, we should certainly have had more. Generally speaking, one effect of an audience in an experiment is to make the performer more than usually cautious, especially if the audience contains a number of people who are unfamiliar, and especially if the performer knows that the audience can check what he is reporting by a direct reference to the original. Outside of an experiment a reporter is very often principally interested in the sort of effect he can produce on those who hear him, and the result is a strong tendency to exaggeration and invention, especially when no easy check-up is possible.

It may seem as if the type of experiment which has just been described and illustrated is bound to exaggerate both the number and the nature of the changes occurring in recall. Certainly it will produce much more radical alteration in a short space of time than will normally happen if only one person is concerned. Yet if we look over the records again we shall see that every report introduces changes, and that some of them are surprisingly complete. To show all that individual remembering is capable of in this way takes a lot of time, for in particular the first occasion upon which anything is remembered exercises a strong and durable influence upon most subsequent occasions, and, of course, every occasion for the use of remembering is in a sort of a way additional practice in what is alleged to be the original material. But, in fact, if the gaps are long enough, and the whole experiment is protracted enough, pretty well the same things happen in individual recall at long term, as can be shown to happen quickly with the kind of connected recall that we have been studying.

6. HOW THE MIND REMEMBERS

It is curious that most people who have been interested in trying to find out how remembering works have started from the special case of learning by heart. Let us try to see what sort of ideas we get if we begin from the much more usual case of remembering in everyday life. It would seem as if this must be the basic process, and every form more definite than this must have grown out of it in response to special circumstances.

One thing is clear enough immediately. We do not ordinarily see or hear something and then form automatically a set of traces which we store away somewhere in the mind, and then bring them out again when they seem to be needed, exactly as they were when they went into store. What we do is to go on building up all the time, throughout the whole of our waking life, a mass of more or less organized experience, the items of which are always liable to affect one another and change one another in many ways. So if we speak of "traces" in the mind which are used when we remember, we have got to think of them rather like lesson material that is being constantly revised, and each time it is revised new material is apt to be added and old material dropped out or altered.

At the same time it is equally clear that we do not build up just one big mass of rather muddled material. We carry what we build with us, and remember it, when we need it, in large working groups which, more than anything else, follow the lines of the interests which we develop. Games experiences go into one group and work experiences into another, and both these very large groups get sub-divided into many others according to our special interests in particular kinds of games or work.

Why do we ordinarily have to use remembering at all? It is because the experiences of the past are useful to help us to deal with the problems or demands of the present. But the circumstances of the present are never exactly the same as those of the past, and its demands, except in special and rather artificial cases, are also very rarely indeed the same demands. And so, more often than not, what we want to do is to reconstruct the past, not simply to repeat it.

But it is not only the material of experience that gets organized into these living, growing and changing masses, but also normally the interests themselves which play the chief part in this organization get connected together. We may, for example, develop a tremendous interest in cricket, and some day see a film in which a cricket match has a place. Then if later on somebody starts speaking about either films or cricket we may remember this particular picture and talk about it as our part in the conversation. Or we may be playing in a cricket match ourselves and put in a stroke which is our version of one we saw in the film. Almost certainly if we saw the film again, and could make a fair comparison, we should find that both our story and our stroke had got mixed up with other events; and they were not strictly repetition at all. Because different interests can and do deal with the same material the possibility of change and development of that material become vastly extended.

It may happen that particular interests get so strong that they sweep all the others away. When that happens to anybody we usually speak of him as "lop-sided," or "biased" or, in some instances, "narrow-minded." When material comes along which cannot be dealt with by the key interest, it is either immediately transformed or else forgotten. But the chances of change in the material that remains alive for an individual of this kind are reduced, and it may be that he is either more literally accurate, or at least more uniform, in what he remembers than most of us.

Or again an interest may in various ways get cut off from all others. The material dealt with by the disconnected interest then remains much less affected by anything else, and when it is remembered is remembered in a more repetitive style. In the very extreme cases a person will go on doing or saying the same things over and over and over again.

Now perhaps we can begin to see why it is that when we know that we shall be expected to repeat things or actions literally and exactly we are forced to adopt special devices, for which we have special names, like "learning by heart." Actually what we really try to do in all such cases is to build up some special kind of interest which will take care of the material that has to be learned and keep it for as long as it is needed in a kind of watertight compartment. Very often it is an "examination interest," or an interest in satisfying a particular teacher, or may be an interest in some debate or discussion. The more we keep an interest to itself, the more likely it is that remembering within the sphere of this interest will be repetitive and literal. Most of us find this very difficult, and no wonder; we have to use other special devices as well, like the verse, and the song, and the dance, and the particular tricks called "mnemonics." And even then the custom of everyday life will be too strong for us, and changes will creep in, though we may believe that we have made no change whatever.

Exactly how the mind, or the central nervous system, can carry about all the organized massed material which it certainly is able to use when necessary, it is exceedingly difficult to understand. For some reason, many people seem to consider it a simpler notion that the mind should hold within itself from day to day millions of copies of the great majority, or perhaps all, of the events that have happened to it. If it could be shown that remembering is nothing but a combination of repetitive reproduction with forgetting, perhaps this would be a simpler notion. But very nearly every experiment on remembering that can be performed, and nearly every observation about remembering that can be made in the course of daily life, shows us that the details that remain when all forgetting is allowed for, change and go on changing for a long time. The notion of millions of copies, remaining ready to be used again and again, except for gaps, contains nothing that is applicable to the facts of the case. All we can say is that, whenever remembering occurs, what is remembered bears a mark of something that is not happening now, but must be treated as if it did happen some time or other; and that however much change has taken place a "family likeness" persists, or could be seen to persist if we had a record of the course of successive changes. There is, in fact, some enduring scheme, or topic, or pattern, but within this the details will undergo many transformations, all of them, often efficiently but sometimes misleadingly, serving the demands of whatever it may be that at any moment makes a person remember.

As a matter of fact, remembering, like any other activity of mind, is not to be thought of, so to speak, as shut up in itself. It grows out of observation, and it is used to help us to solve problems as we meet them. Its investigation leads us directly to our final topic of discussion; what happens when the mind thinks.

7. SUMMARY

1. It is easy to show that many things which are alleged to be directly observed are in fact introduced as a result of earlier experiences and so are remembered.

2. Formal experiments on "learning by heart" show that there is a normal and regular "curve of forgetting" and that:

(*a*) With all material, but especially with meaningless material there tends to be a large amount of early forgetting.

(*b*) "Effort to remember" seems often to result in rapid immediate forgetting.

(*c*) The position of items, or material, in a sequence which has to be remembered has much to do with recall, early and late positions being the most favourable.

(*d*) Sleep may arrest forgetting, and so perhaps prolong the chance of accurate recall.

(*e*) To some extent people can, at the time of learning, determine for how long they are going to be able to remember accurately.

(*f*) With longish, or fairly difficult verbal material,

distributed practice in the learning stage appears generally to be more economical than massed practice.

(*g*) This may, however, be connected with a natural tendency for interrupted tasks, or tasks which are left incomplete, to be taken up again as soon as time and circumstances allow.

3. Everyday remembering is very rarely a matter of exact repetition, and it would not be at all useful if it were. For we remember things that have happened in one set of circumstances to help us to solve problems that arise in a different set.

4. The quickest and most obvious way of showing the tremendous changes that normally take place in everyday remembering is to carry out an experiment on serial recall in which a number of people take part one after another. Much the same amount and degree of transformation, however, do occur in repeated individual recall, though the process may be long drawn-out.

5. If we try to form a picture of what happens to make remembering, in the form in which it generally occurs, possible, we have to think of the material of experience as being all the time organized and reorganized into large groups, mainly by the operation of a number of related special interests. Ordinary remembering is far less a matter of repetition, which demands the adoption of special learning devices, than of reconstruction.

6. If by a "good memory" we mean a capacity for accurate and literal recall, its secret is a lot of hard work in the learning stage, and a development of interests, each of which is highly self-contained and cut off from others. If, as is reasonable, by "good memory" we mean remembering what is most generally useful in helping us to adapt ourselves readily to the demands of life as they occur, its secret lies in the organization of experience through the operation of all-round interests which are closely linked together.

CHAPTER SIX

The Mind Thinks

When a person remembers anything, he is using information which he has picked up from one set of circumstances to help him in dealing with another set. Indeed, there may be no mental process that does not in some way link up one situation with another, using material and information that has already been acquired to settle problems which still have to be solved.

Is it then the case that any normal individual will naturally, and without making any particular effort, transfer whatever he learns in one situation to any other situation that may crop up in which it could be of use? This is an old problem, which nearly everybody must have discussed at some time or another. Does training and consequent learning in one field or subject help, or hinder, learning in another field or subject?

1. TRANSFER OF TRAINING

It used to be generally supposed, and still sometimes is, that there are some subjects which are particularly likely to be a help in the learning of other subjects. So far as school training was concerned, the two that were always picked out, on the ground that skill in them would be most easily transferred to build up skill in other fields, were Classics and Mathematics. There have always been people, however, who have held that there is little real evidence to show that these subjects are any better than some others, if they are to be considered good in proportion as they can help students to learn other things.

What is the evidence about transfer? The easiest case

to study experimentally is the one where a person learns to make a series of bodily movements and then is transferred to a different problem, which, however, requires him to make some, at least, of the same movements over again. Suppose, for example, an animal or a person is trained to run a maze in which he must go along every second turning from beginning to end. If he is now confronted with a maze in which he has to go along every third turning to get to the end, will the initial training make the second learning longer or shorter?

A vast number of experiments have been designed and carried out on this model. Very often it is said that there is evidence for automatic transfer, positive or negative, depending directly on the amount of similarity in detail that there is between the learning and the test situation. Suppose, for example, a maze, or a list of words, is fully learned, and then the learner is given the same maze, or the same list, over again. The positive "transfer"—but it seems rather silly to use the word at all in this case—is complete within certain time limits. But as the second maze or list contains more and more new items of movement or words, negative transfer, or interference between the two processes of learning, increases up to a point, and then diminishes once more. Finally, when the two mazes or lists have no common elements at all, neither interferes with the other; but whether the first learning can help the second still remains undecided.

Even if all this were much more definitely established than it in fact is, it would be of very little service for any purpose whatsoever. For, except under artificial and carefully arranged conditions, it is hard to tell how much any subject or skill overlaps another one. To count the number of apparently identical elements can be most misleading, since, as we have seen over and over again, the character of any item in a series is strongly influenced by its relation to the preceding and following items.

Let us try a rather different type of experiment. Get seven small electric light bulbs, mount them on a block of wood and wire them up, but with concealed connections, to seven switches. Arrange the circuits so that the lamps can be lighted only in a certain order. For example, reading from left to right, bulb 1 is lighted by switch 2; bulb 1 is extinguished and bulb 7 lighted by switch 4, and the subsequent connections are: bulb 2 by switch 6; bulb 6 by switch 1; bulb 3 by switch 3; bulb 5 by switch 5; and bulb 4 by switch 7. Now take a second 7 bulbs and switches, and arrange the connections so that exactly the same order of relation of switches is used, but the starting switch is a different one.

Get two groups of operators. With the first setting the instructions to both groups will be exactly the same:

"Starting with the bulb on the extreme left you have to find which switches to use to light each bulb once and none more than once, finishing with the bulb in the middle. The lights may come on in any order so long as each bulb is used once only and the last one is in the middle."

With the second setting the instructions to one group will be exactly the same as for the first setting. To the other group you will say: "The task is exactly the same as before. The correct order of switches may be different but the scheme of arrangement of the order is precisely the same as in the first setting."

Both groups have to solve their first problem by trial and error. Note the time taken by each operator and what he does.

With the second problem one group is given no additional clue. A few operators will almost certainly turn up who, having by trial discovered the starting switch for the second setting, will go on at once to try the same principle of arrangement of switches. But probably there will be only a few of these, and in this group of operators the time taken for solution and the number of apparently blind trials made will not differ much from the first setting of the problem.

The other group will, in the main, show an entirely different kind of behaviour. Having found the starting switch by trial they will transfer from the first situation and solve the problem forthwith.

This is, of course, a very simple case, but it is easily possible to complicate it to any desired degree both with this and with other kinds of material. The results will almost certainly remain consistent with these. If a particular problem, subject matter, or skill, is so taught that the only point emphasized is mastery of that, what is learned will remain in most cases severely tied up with the initial conditions, and there will be little or no positive transfer. There may, however, be quite a lot of interference if even a slightly different problem, subject matter, or skill has to be attempted.

As we have already discovered (see pp. 63–5) it is in general much easier to notice differences and the points of difference between situations, than to notice likenesses and the precise points of likeness. So if we have to turn from learning in one situation to learning in another one, unless special guidance has been given us during the initial learning, we are likely to be impressed by the differences or, if we look for likenesses, to fail to identify them correctly. The natural thing then is either to take the new subject or problem as something to be learned on its own account, or we get muddled between the two and the first interferes with the second.

The most fundamental thing about transfer is that if it is desired it must, as a rule, be sought and prepared for in the style of instruction or teaching. So long as the emphasis is upon the particular material or problem that is to be studied the scales are weighted against any positive transfer. If stress is laid upon the principles of construction of the material, or on the manner in which the components of a skill contribute to the task set, the balance is tipped in favour of the maximum positive transfer and the minimum interference.

There are two other things. The first is that if we have two tasks, one more difficult and one easier, and it looks as if learning either ought to help us to learn the other, we should start by learning the more difficult one. There is evidence for example that people who begin with the more difficult of the two winding tasks described on p. 47, master the easier one more quickly; but people who begin with the easier one gain nothing at all in the learning of the more difficult. It is not hard to see reasons why this should happen, but a lot more experiment is needed to show whether it is generally true or not. The second thing is that if we could only produce people who would go about looking for likenesses, instead of allowing themselves to be struck by differences, we should perhaps do more for transfer than could be done in any other way. Nearly all the great advances, whether in knowledge or in skill, have been won by bringing together problems and methods of solution of problems that have before remained apart. There is a lot more to be said about this, however, for it is not simply noticing likenesses that counts but being able to pick out the right ones.

We can now go back for a moment to the old question of whether Classics and Mathematics are a kind of superior school subject because they help us, more than any other subjects, to learn a great many other things. Perhaps we can say that they are more likely to help students in this way who find them very difficult than students who find them easy. But, except that probably most students do find them difficult, there is not much satisfaction in that. If they have any such superiority it is because, each in its own sphere, the classical languages with words, and mathematics with numbers and numerical ideas, can be used readily to illustrate principles—of construction, of relation and of analysis. This, however, is a matter of the style of instruction adopted and not of the nature of the subject itself, for pretty well all the other school subjects can be taught and learned in this way if the attempt is made. If Greek, Latin and Mathematics are simply studied as self-contained subjects, and only, or mainly, to achieve mastery in them, they will have no more general significance than learning in any other field of knowledge could have.

Often it has been said that the outstanding superiority of these particular subjects is that they teach their students to think. If in fact they were bound to do this, however the instruction was given or taken, the statement would be true. But are they? This question leads at once to the last and perhaps the most important of all the problems of these lectures. What do we do when we think? And what kinds of training are most likely to produce the effective and efficient thinker?

2. INTELLIGENCE AND THINKING

In the year 1897 the aldermen of the German town of Breslau became worried about the distribution of the hours of study in their schools. It happened that they had an unusually sensible Professor of Psychology in their University, Herman Ebbinghaus, who as we have seen already invented the method of experimenting about remembering with material which put everybody on a level to begin with, and to him they went for advice. Whether he directly solved their problems for them is not known, but what he did has had the most tremendous consequences, whether more for good or ill, for pleasure or for pain, perhaps others can decide. He thought that the hours of study ought to be in some way relative to the intelligence of the student, and he invented and soon afterwards published the first formal test of intelligence.

He selected a few stories, or fables, and had them printed so that in each line a number of words or short phrases were missed out. The test was to fill up the blank spaces, and it speedily became known as the "Ebbinghaus Completion Test."

As everybody knows, inventing intelligence tests has almost achieved the rank of a sport, and there must be few psychologists or teachers who have not played at it at some time or another. The form of straightforward completion is not now often adopted, but the principle of filling up gaps remains perhaps the most important of all the general features in the construction of formal tests of intelligence.

Now, of course, whatever intelligence may be held to include, it covers other processes besides that of an ability to think. Yet every intelligent person is supposed to be a person who can think if the occasion arises. It is therefore of great interest that the first formal intelligence test should have been a direct exercise in the filling up of gaps, and that capacity to do this should have continued to be demanded by all subsequent developments of such tests. For no doubt it will have been noticed that in all our discussions and experiments, whenever the mind comes into operation, most unmistakably it is by filling up gaps that are left in the evidence that has been gained by direct observation.

3. FILLING UP GAPS

We began by asking how the human senses and judgment can make reasonably exact measures or estimates of distance, size, length, breadth, height, direction and speed of movement and the like. We found that absolute measures and estimates, given to a single magnitude, are not likely to be correct. Relative magnitudes are much better dealt with, and best of all are the cases where we can use standard scales, with fixed points arranged in a systematic order. Accuracy, however, does not go on increasing indefinitely with more and more fixed points. In many cases (see p. 24) it is better to leave a gap between two marked points and to let the mind estimate the position of a recorder within the gap.

Then we considered skilled movements of various kinds. The same principles were illustrated. Why is it that the position, distance, distribution, direction and speed of movement, and resistance of controls on machines have a great influence upon the efficiency with which the machine can be operated? Why is it that all the leading strokes in an active game have their "key" characters? It must be because any efficient sequence of bodily movements falls naturally into a standard group in agreement with the fundamental mechanics of body and mind. If we cut short any skill sequence we find that the performer is already, so to speak, set towards the next move. At any moment in a skilled performance, that is to say, the good performer is ready to fill up a prospective gap. He may not be able to describe in words what is coming next, but he can produce it in action, and all the time until the skilled action is complete he is using the incomplete evidence which his senses have picked up from signals in the environment and from his preceding moves, to assist him to carry on the moves to their desired end.

Our study of perception and observation told us the same story. Very rarely indeed, if ever, are all the details that are reported to have been observed literally appreciated at the time by the senses. We pick up bits of direct evidence, leave gaps, and fill up the gaps, usually without knowing that there are any, in what seems to be an appropriate way. This we can do because we are always drawing upon more or less standardized groupings of evidence, and not treating the items that our senses pick out as separate and self-contained. But in this case both where the gaps occur and their extent vary much more from instance to instance and there is much more freedom in the ways in which they are filled.

Connecting things or events together which occur at different points in a succession is obviously and directly a process of filling up an interval in the evidence. And here also the interval is filled in accordance with standard relationships that are somehow immediately appreciated by the mind, or have been learned in the course of experience, or are partly the one and partly the other.

Then we came to remembering, and we found that this takes place when something happens which leaves us unable to do what is required unless we can reinforce it in some way. We may be able to fill up the gap by drawing upon the materials of evidence which we have ourselves accumulated earlier. These materials are not arranged in a haphazard way, or even, as a rule, in a straightforward succession, just as they did in fact occur. They are built into groups by the interests which we carry about with us. Such groups, again, are a kind of standard which we can and must use to help us to deal with fresh items of experience as they come along. Only they are not fixed standards like the scales and their intervals. They go with us from day to day, growing and changing, most of them, all the time.

We can see that we have not been considering a number of separate and disconnected processes. From the simplest to the most complex of all the processes that we have studied, the mind, working together directly or indirectly with the senses that yield it its direct evidence, proceeds by the same principles. First the mind does not seem to be able, at any stage, to deal satisfactorily with isolated magnitudes, disconnected items of bodily movement, single sets of sensory qualities, or events of any kind taken entirely by themselves. Its great function is to deal with these when they leave some sort of a gap, and it cannot fill up the gap satisfactorily either to itself or to the structure of human knowledge, unless it can use standards, comparisons, and have access to evidence additional to that which is directly contributed on the spot, by its senses.

4. INTERPOLATION AND EXTRAPOLATION

Not all the gaps of which we have been speaking are alike, and not all the processes required to fill them up are alike either. If we take one of the two simplest of our instances, the estimation of a position between two fixed marks, the gap has direct available evidence on both sides and we interpolate a solution. If we take the other one, the move to the next item in a skill, we have to consider the direct available evidence as complete up to a point and then stopping short, and we must extrapolate a solution. Nothing like enough is known about these two processes of interpolating and extrapolating, and it should be well worth while for somebody to think out all sorts of instances and try them as experiments under controlled conditions. On the face of it, it seems as if interpolation should be the simpler and easier process; and it certainly is the case that what most people are willing to call thinking is concerned with carrying further evidence that is complete only up to a point, that is with extrapolation. No doubt this is because most cases of interpolating with which we have to deal seem to mean either relying upon some fixed standard of differences which apparently everybody must use, as in our case of measurement, or upon some use of remembering to join up the two ends of the gap.

It is not really as simple as all this of course. For example, take a gap like this ——— ———. The interval could be filled in any sort of way. But if somebody, being given no additional information, filled it with an eccentric design, our principal conclusion would certainly be that he had an odd and fanciful mind, and we should certainly be inclined to consider that he was in some way neglecting the evidence.

Suppose, however, the gap is a very large one. The situation has changed. There is some stage in an increasing size of interval at which it becomes reasonable or necessary to fill it up by a number of steps each related to the next. If we meet a friend after a long interval and notice that his appearance has changed, we often try to fill up the blank space in some way that will account for what has happened. We have two bits of evidence at either end of a gap, but there is a great amount of freedom in the filling. We usually take the start of the process as an effort of imagination and all the rest, since there must be some consistency in the story, as imaginative thinking.

There are different cases, of which this, for example, is one:

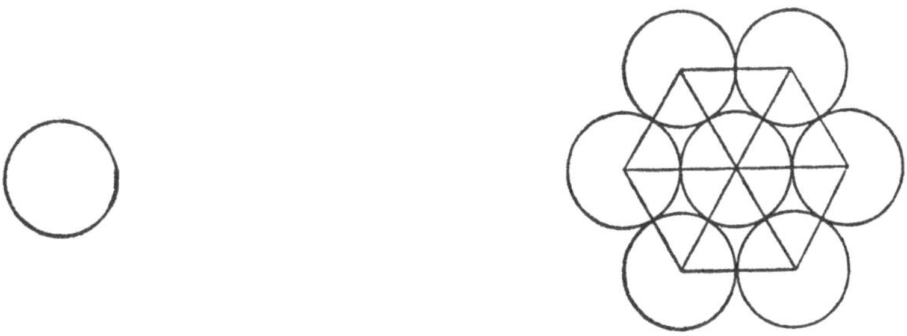

FIG. 27.

Here we appear bound to work within a particular system, and every step follows necessarily upon every other and even the order of steps is nearly, though not quite, necessary. Probably everybody would agree to call this process of interpolation a thinking process proper and unalloyed.

It would seem, then, that thinking can be treated as a process of filling up gaps by a series of steps, in accordance with incomplete evidence that is appreciated by our senses; that the steps must be consistent with one another;

that when we have to use the materials of day by day experience there is a good deal of freedom about the step we pick out to start from, and for this we use imagination; and that when we work in some definite system, especially of numerical, spatial or temporal relations, every step, the connection from one step to another, and to some extent the order of the steps, are to be regarded as necessary. We can perhaps get a little farther still by considering in more detail the case of extrapolation. This is the case in which evidence stops short at some point and we are asked to continue it further. It is by far the commonest of all cases in which thinking is stimulated in everyday life. We must try a few experiments. Take the following figure:

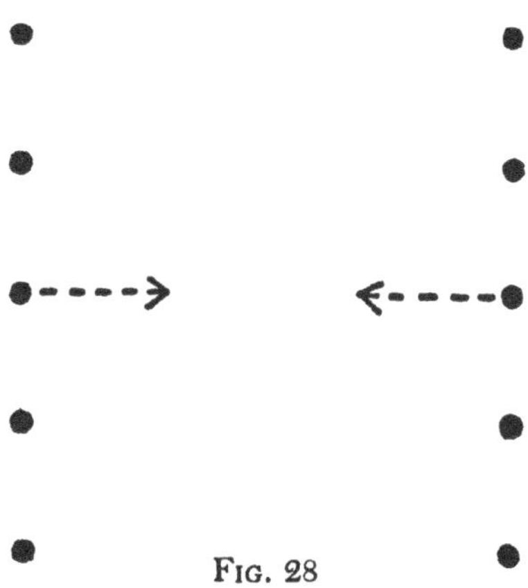

Fig. 28

and ask any observer to treat it as the first figure in a set and to construct the next one. Almost anything can happen; there is no clear clue. It is true that, owing to the conventional meaning of arrow-heads it is probable that the observer will shift the positions of the middle dots in each vertical line. But how far will he move them? He need not move anything. He could introduce new arrow-heads, or new dots; or just as well he could drop them out. He could, and in fact he will, do any one of a large number of different things so long as he keeps to a design of dots. There is great freedom and the exercise is principally one of imagination.

Now add a second figure:

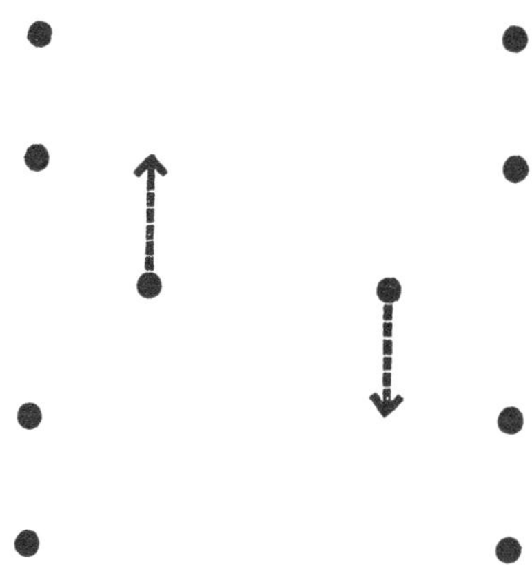

FIG. 29.

At once the whole situation changes. The great majority of observers will proceed with confidence to

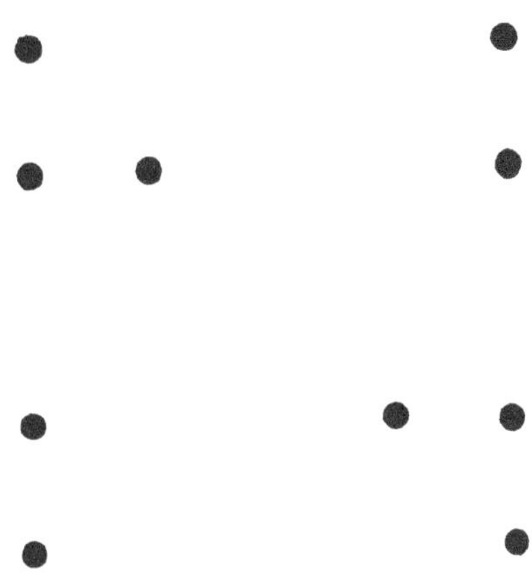

FIG. 30.

From this point you may go on, and, providing you use the same principle, produce almost any variety of the basic design you please. Some observers may need more than two steps of evidence, but there will come a point beyond which absolutely everybody who is prepared to accept the rules of the game, and who is not mentally deficient, will work with increasing confidence, speed and unanimity.

It seems fair to say that in order to extrapolate into a gap there must be at least two items which are treated as evidence, and in complicated cases there may have to be more than two. These two or more items are used in order to extract a principle, or rule, according to which the so-far incomplete instance is carried further. It is tempting to say that if the observer has to draw upon his own experience for one of the sources of evidence he always has some degree of freedom, and his choice involves what would be called imagination rather than thinking. But we must consider other types of instance, where evidence that can be observed in some way through the senses has to be used to solve a definite problem which has only one correct answer, or a limited number.

On page 129 is shown the famous Horse and Rider puzzle. The oblong strip containing the riders has to be superimposed upon the square strip containing the horses in such a way that there will be a rider astride upon each horse in the proper position. Neither strip must be broken, bent, torn or cut.

If you do not already know the solution, make a copy of the drawing with horses and riders on separate slips, and try the puzzle. Find other people who do not know it and get them to try.

Sometimes, but rather rarely, the solution is achieved in the course of an almost random moving about of the strips into all sorts of different positions. More frequently the answer, if it is reached at all, is obtained in a sudden flash, and by a process that we seem bound to call "insight" or "intuition," not by "thinking it out." Either the square strip must be turned through an angle of ninety degrees and pushed under the oblong, or the oblong turned the same amount and put over the square.

Much the most interesting thing about this case is that it requires a completely revolutionary change in a way of looking at the objects involved. Nobody ever ordinarily sees the front legs of one horse as belonging

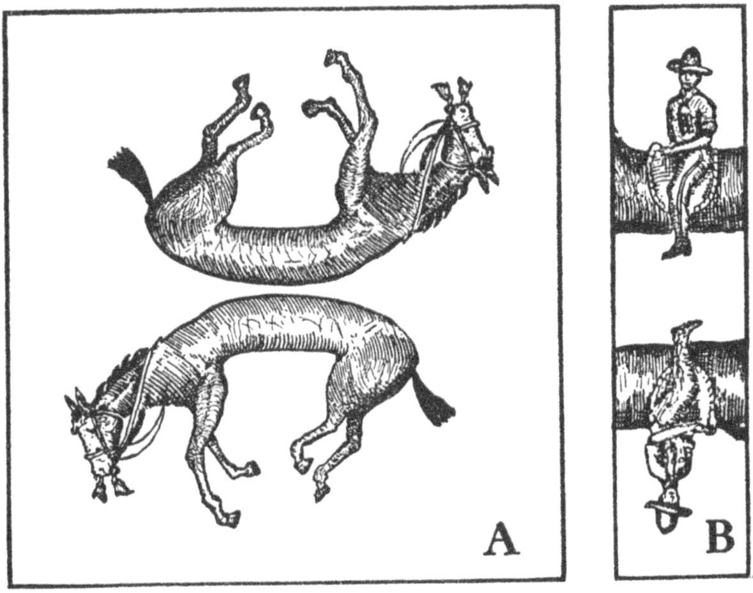

FIG. 31.

to the back legs of another, and that is what we have to do here. It may well be that whenever any radical change has to be effected in a normal manner of looking at anything, if it is achieved at all, it must be achieved either by laborious trial and error or by the sudden flash of insight. Many of the world's most brilliant inventions do appear to have been made in this intuitive manner.

Compare this with the variety of rope and ring puzzle which is depicted in Fig. 32.

One of the rings must be moved from one large loop to the other.

It is easy to make a model of any desired size. Do so and try to get the solution and let others try also who are

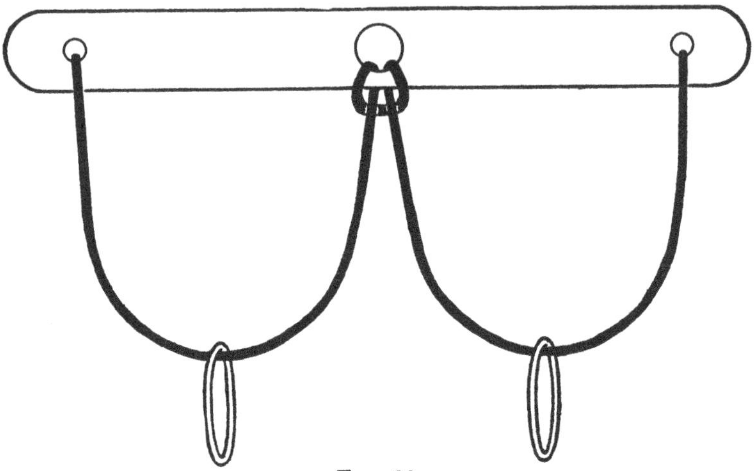

FIG. 32.

not familiar with this type of problem. It seems practically impossible to get the required answer by mere random moves. Also hardly anybody, if anybody, sees the whole solution in a single flash. The steps required are:

(*a*) Move the ring up to the hole.

(*b*) The ring will not pass through the hole: the wooden strip will not pass through the ring: the ends of the loops must not be detached: only one possibility remains: the little loop must be passed through the hole. Do this.

(*c*) Move the ring round the little loop.

(*d*) Move the little loop back through the hole.

(*e*) The ring is now on the big loop. Let it slip down to meet the other ring.

(*c*) and (*d*) may present some difficulty, even when it

is realized that they are what must be done, and may be achieved only after some actively directed trial. In this instance, we find the same factors as in some of our cases of interpolation. The process goes by steps. Every step has to be treated as the necessary consequence of its predecessor. At no stage in this is there any radical revision of a normal kind of observation. All the items that must be attended to occur, and must be treated in the same ways as in other situations. The required or appropriate points of agreement with other instances must be selected, and that is where the main difficulty lies. If that is done, the whole series can be understood as a necessary one, and is the same for all operators.

We will consider briefly one other illustration of extrapolation which is tied up with a definite problem, this time with a more general problem still. According to a story, when Catherine the Great was rebuilding St. Petersburg, as it was then called, she had a whim that the streets of the city must all be laid out in such a way that she could drive from her palace and along the whole of the road-ways of the city without ever passing along any stretch of any street more than once. She did not object to crossing-over points, but she must be able to plan trips in the city, covering either the whole or selected sections, without going more than once along any particular road or stretch of road, other than the one from the palace into the city itself. According to the story the chief architect tried and failed, but the problem was solved by a famous mathematician of the time.

All that is needed is the application of a simple commonsense principle which anybody can understand. But not many people seem to hit upon the principle by analysing the general requirements alone. We can therefore consider the instance as one in which evidence which is in itself incomplete may be used to achieve an issue which is both certain and general.

Choose by inspection which of the following designs satisfy the requirement that, starting from the black oblong, it is possible to go over every part of the pattern without ever traversing any section more than once.

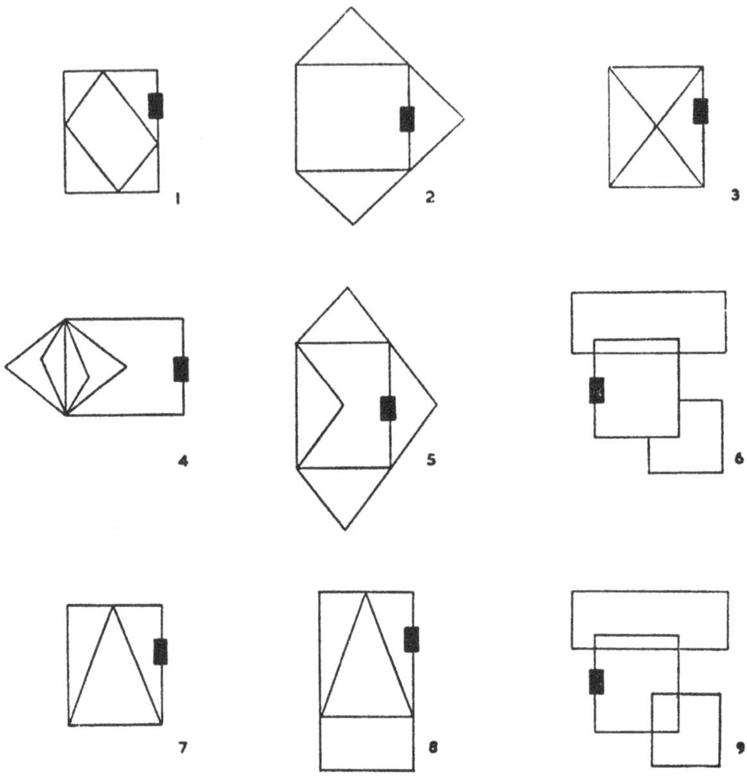

FIG. 33.

Obviously the condition that we want to find must be illustrated in some feature or features which all of the patterns that satisfy the requirements possess, and none of the others possesses.

See if you can discover what that feature, or those features, must be, and whether, when you have done this, it becomes clear at once how the important feature, or features, can be expressed as a completely general solution of the problem.

The required selection is Nos. 1, 4, 5, 6, 8. The critical points of agreement are that in all of these, and in none of the rest, whenever a road junction is reached there are an even number of possibilities, except at the starting point of the journey, and this is only a formal exception because at the starting point also there is a way back which is not identical with any way out.

As soon as these points are picked out it becomes clear that they give the necessary and sufficient solution. For if roads meet, at any place except the beginning, every time the meeting place is visited there must be a special way to it and a different way from it.

This illustration will also probably make it clearer than any of the others that we have considered that the greatest difficulty, when evidence has to be collected from instances not quite complete in themselves and carried further, is in the identification of the critical points of agreement and disagreement between the instances. Even in this rather simple case as it is here illustrated there are other points of agreement: all the roads are straight, the sizes of all the angles and the number of ways into and out of junctions lie within certain limits. In most experimental fields, where we must have a large number of instances to deal with, there are far more points of agreement than important points of agreement, and prominent items may be widely distributed without being present in all instances. We must also not suppose that there is thinking only when the result finally reached is the correct one.

5. EVERYDAY THINKING

In all of the illustrations that we have considered in detail the gaps that are present can be closed in one way which must be admitted to be correct, or in other ways which can be identified as incorrect. Many people have supposed that all thinking must be capable of being treated in this way, and so, if they have made any attempt to experiment about the process, they have set problems which can be shown to have one right answer and an indefinite number of wrong ones. When this is done it becomes fatally easy to go a step farther and to suppose that we think only if we arrive at correct issues.

There are plenty of instances, most common of all in everyday life, in which we know the evidence up to a point and extrapolate further to an issue, but this issue remains one only of several possible issues for each of which about as much might be said. We can try experiments by constructing a narrative up to a point, leaving it unfinished and then asking anybody we like to accept the evidence we give him and carry it further. Here is a case:

A GOOD OPPORTUNITY

"So that's the chap, is it?" said Gray. He was looking at a small photograph.

"Yes," said White; "there he is; the most dangerous man in Europe to-day. For the moment he's disappeared, run to ground. But we're pretty sure he's safe and he'll turn up again somewhere, some day. If he isn't stopped there'll be another flaming great war sooner or later; the biggest yet."

"Look," said Gray, "what would you do if he turned up here to-night?"

"Do?" replied White. "I'd just arrange a nice fatal accident for him. It would be easy enough. We're in the depths of the country. It's very dark and foggy. Nobody else would ever know. It'd be perfectly safe. And it would be a thoroughly good deed."

"Well, I'm not so sure," said Gray. "You mightn't, you know, if it came to the point; not that there's the slightest chance it will. But if you did I'd be tempted to help. How would you do it, anyway?"

So the two young Englishmen set to work to concoct a plan. They got one, too, and it seemed as safe as houses. When they had finished and were chuckling about it, there came a ring at the door-bell. A moment later two men were shown into the room in which they were sitting.

"Two gentlemen to see you, sir," said the butler; "they seem to have lost their way."

They were foreigners. Gray hastily slipped the photograph between the pages of a book, for one of them had the unmistakable features of the missing man.

Get as many people as you can to agree to accept the evidence as it is stated in this story and then to say what they consider happened next. It is not difficult to make up other instances to the same general pattern, incomplete short stories, arguments or descriptions, and to get them continued, always under the general condition that the evidence as presented is accepted without criticism.

A lot of surprising results have a way of turning up with this sort of experimental material, but we need here consider only the two broadly different processes which come into play. The most common thing to happen of all seems to be that whoever is trying to fill up this kind of gap immediately falls back on some conventional principle or other which he has picked up uncritically perhaps from home, from school, or from some other working or playing social environment. In the case given, for instance, it can be some form of, "Englishmen are always good sports," or "All's fair in politics," or "The biggest step is from idea to action."

The extension given is then practically nothing but putting the generalization into some concrete descriptive form. In this case Gray and White may entertain their unexpected visitor courteously and see him happily off next morning; or they may do what they said they were going to do, with or without success; or they may try the plan but shy off at the last moment.

The less common thing is the selection of some items of the evidence as "key" points; an attempt to remember or construct other cases in which the same key characteristics occur; by a comparison of these to develop a number of related steps leading consistently to an issue in line with whatever part of the evidence was accepted as important.

There are certainly some important differences between thinking with this sort of material and thinking with the sort of material we considered in most of the earlier cases. Some people would deny that the uncritical acceptance of a conventional rule or principle and its description in a concrete form is thinking at all. Beyond a doubt it is a different process from that analytical inspection of well defined properties which, especially, as we have found, in the case of spatial, temporal and numerical relations, may issue in a necessary and universal principle. For the acceptance of a particular convention has always, or almost always, an emotional element attached. Also the illustration of the conventional generalization has neither the range nor the certainty possible in most of the other cases we have discussed in this chapter. But it seems silly to be very sticky about all this, and if we refuse to admit that this is thinking, we rule out a large amount of what goes under this name in ordinary life.

The point that it is important to remember is that in all these instances there are various ways of filling up the gap according to the principle that is accepted or the items of evidence that are developed. Very rarely indeed can we say that one way is right and all the others wrong.

6. THINKING

Although there is much more to be found out by carefully arranged and graded experiments, it is now possible to state what are the fundamental processes involved when we think.

All thinking is directed to filling up gaps either by interpolation or by extrapolation, but not all processes of filling gaps are thinking processes. How many ways there are of doing this we have not attempted to decide, but we have distinguished two. In one the filling is immediately identified or, as we very often say, "seen." This process, at whatever level it occurs, is akin to that insight, or intuition which we found to be a characteristic way of dealing with the Horse and Rider puzzle. It can occur in a good many cases that seem to be very simple, like interpolating in a scale or a set of numbers, or carrying on a skill. In complex instances it seems to be particularly connected with achieving a radically new type of observation or movement or—though we have not discussed this—something really new and original in the combination of meanings. In the other the filling is developed by steps, which are presented and treated as consistent both with the evidence and one with another. Sometimes the steps are regarded as alternative possibilities which are excluded one by one until one only is left, and then this is accepted as satisfactory, or as the best that can be achieved. This occurs, for example, in some cases when readings are interpolated in a scale, or movements finally incorporated in a skill, and it always involves a certain amount of trial and error, though certainly not of blind trial and error. Much more often, especially when the gap is a large one, or when evidence is being expanded beyond the point it has reached, the process is constructive, the first step leading on to all the others.

In this case, if the process is concerned with the properties of numbers, or mainly with spatial or temporal series, or even if it has to do with the meanings of words and statements that have been completely defined and accepted, every step may appear as necessary and the same for all. In all other instances the first step particularly is selected with considerable freedom and we say that imagination is needed. There is, however, always the condition that the first step must be consistent with whatever evidence is available. All further steps must be consistent one with another.

Whenever we try to expand incomplete evidence by thinking we must have at least two items to work on, and we may need many more. This is because thinking must have something of the nature of a rule or a principle to go on. The clearest instances are when we extrapolate as with our dot pattern (p. 126); but exactly the same condition is involved if we have to attempt to fill up a large gap with evidence at either end. The evidence at the starting end now has to be supplemented by some first step that we provide or select for ourselves, and the two (or more) together will give us the line along which we shall eventually reach the evidence at the other end.

This is generally what makes correct thinking a difficult job, especially in experimental science and everyday life. We have to proceed by noticing agreements and disregarding differences, and we have found already (see p. 118) that this is not easy.

Moreover there will usually be a lot of agreements of which we have to use only one or two, and there will often be many differences which occur alike in nearly all the cases but not in quite all, and we must not be led away by these. So whenever the inspection of a large number of instances has to be undertaken, the successful thinker must be well-informed, and he must also possess something for which we have no other word than "wisdom." Also he must not be afraid of hard labour.

Now we may see also that there are two broadly contrasted methods which can be used. When we are dealing with data whose properties are known and the relations of whose properties can be defined at the beginning, we can arrive at a principle by analysis and then use an appropriate instance, or group of instances, to fill up the gap that is waiting. This is deduction. When, as is more common, we cannot enumerate the properties completely and, especially, do not know at the beginning what are their relations, we have to inspect instances and, using agreements and differences, seek some fitting principle of construction through these. This is induction. Some minds seem to be better at the first, some at the second and some, not many, are good at both.

7. TRAINING THE MIND TO THINK

Can minds be trained to think? This is fundamentally the same problem as that of transfer of training, and the answers, in so far as any can be given, are the same answers.

There is no kind of training that will, or can, automatically produce the thinker. The secret lies not in the particular matter of instruction but in the style of it. We have to produce people who will go about the world looking for agreements, even in the most unlikely quarters, and refusing to be overmuch worried by those differences that spring at once to observation. It is very rarely possible to do this in terms of one subject matter only, or of subject matters that are kept apart in the learning stage. As in thinking we need to have more than one item in order to detect some rule or principle to use in further development, so it seems that we must usually bring together more than one subject to put a learner on the way to become a thinker.

When we raise the question of training to think, however, what we really mean is: Can the mind be trained to think successfully and fruitfully? Now we have seen that thinking characteristically proceeds by a series of steps which are consistent one with the next and all in line with whatever evidence there may be. So far as consistency goes there are a lot of possible errors to which the mind seems particularly prone. They have been collected and classified by the older logicians under the name of "fallacies." Merely learning these as rules of logic will by itself do nothing at all. But learning them linked with and illustrated in whatever related fields of subject matter are being taught, will do a lot, and the right age is fairly early. So far as loyalty to evidence is concerned this can certainly be taught by precept, example and demonstration, and it will rarely be learned in any other ways.

But this is not all. By far the most important capacity required is to be able to select and use those points of agreement in a sufficient number of cases which can be developed so that the gap that is waiting will be completely closed and at the same time, since the pursuit of knowledge is unending, further gaps, lying beyond, will be opened. Wisdom is needed, and is perhaps a peculiar kind of sensitivity to the clues that are worth exploring and to the others whose exploration will merely lead to a wilderness of trouble. Beyond doubt wisdom must be acquired and is a fruit, usually, of prolonged experience and a wide range of closely related interests. Yet not everybody who possesses both of these appears to be wise. If only we could discover for certain the differences between those who, being given about the same opportunities, acquire wisdom and those who do not, perhaps we could say whether we could plan with success to produce the wise thinker. As it is there is nothing for it but to admit that nobody knows.

SUMMARY

1. The effects of training are not automatically transferred from one situation to another, except in so far as interference goes. Positive transfer requires a special style of instruction.

2. So far as present evidence goes the instruction required must call attention to the principles of construction or arrangement of whatever is being learned and get the learner to be on the look-out for similar rules in other settings.

3. There is also some evidence that transfer is more likely to be made from the relatively difficult to the relatively easy than from the relatively easy to the relatively difficult.

4. All thinking involves transfer, for thinking is essentially the filling up of gaps.

5. The process may be one of interpolation in which there is evidence on both sides of the gap and the filling may be by a single step, or by development from one step to another if the gap is a large one.

6. Alternatively, if the evidence is complete to a point but must be carried further, the process is one of extrapolation. Here also there may be a single step, illustrating either a necessary principle or an accepted convention, or exclusion of all steps but one, or progressive development of a series of steps.

7. In every case the filling must be in line with the evidence provided or with selected parts of it, and if there are several steps they must be consistent one with another.

8. When the gap occurs in a system all of whose properties can be fully defined, every step, and when there are several, to some extent the order of the steps, appear as necessary.

9. When such definition is not possible, as almost always in the arts and in everyday life and generally in branches of experimental science, there is a good deal of freedom in the selection of the first step, and, within the limits of consistency, of any others as well.

10. If the gap can be filled only by a very radical change in any ordinary way of looking at the evidence available, it seems as if there must be either laborious trial and error or a sudden flash of insight or intuition.

11. In other cases it is often necessary to inspect a number, and sometimes a large number of instances, and thinking then builds principally upon alleged agreements among them all.

12. The process of thinking cannot be adequately studied by confining the attention to problems which can be shown to have only one correct solution.

13. The successful thinker must be able to observe accurately, to avoid being discouraged by apparent differences, or being misled by likenesses which are common to many instances but not to all. Also, he must be able to select those points of agreement which can be used to close the gap, and at the same time, in most instances, to open up new gaps. And he must decide when he has inspected a sufficient number of cases. He needs, therefore, not only capacity to think but capacity to think wisely.

14. Minds can be trained to think in the same ways and to the same degree that they can be trained to transfer skill from one situation to another. They can also be trained to avoid common errors in passing from one step to another in a process of thinking. But nobody so far has discovered how by training to produce wisdom.

INDEX

For Product Safety Concerns and Information please contact our EU representative GPSR@taylorandfrancis.com Taylor & Francis Verlag GmbH, Kaufingerstraße 24, 80331 München, Germany